Robert Bridges

Suppressed Chapters and other Bookishness

Robert Bridges

Suppressed Chapters and other Bookishness

ISBN/EAN: 9783743328914

Manufactured in Europe, USA, Canada, Australia, Japa

Cover: Foto ©Thomas Meinert / pixelio.de

Manufactured and distributed by brebook publishing software (www.brebook.com)

Robert Bridges

Suppressed Chapters and other Bookishness

SUPPRESSED CHAPTERS

AND OTHER BOOKISHNESS

BY

ROBERT BRIDGES

AUTHOR OF "OVERHEARD IN ARCADY"

NEW YORK
CHARLES SCRIBNER'S SONS
1895

CONTENTS

Suppressed Chapters

	PAGE
A New Dolly Dialogue,	3
Trilby's Christmas,	7
Narcissus and Hesper on Wheels,	11
Little Wayoff,	15
Lost Chords,	18
Buy the Idiot Brand,	21
Some Remarks of Major Brace,	24

Arcadian Letters

To Terence Mulvaney,	29
To Evadne Galbraith,	32
To Diana of the Crossways, Surrey,	36
To One who is Tired of Reading,	40
To Jean at Twenty-two,	43
To a Certain Critic,	46
To a Friend Starting on a Vacation,	49

Novels that Everybody Read

	PAGE
Lord Ormont and his Aminta,	55
The Manxman,	58
Trilby,	61
Tess of the D'Urbervilles,	65
The Prisoner of Zenda,	68
Ships that Pass in the Night,	71
Katharine Lauderdale,	74
The Jungle Book,	78
Pembroke,	81
David Balfour,	84

The Literary Partition of Scotland

The Literary Partition of Scotland,	89
J. M. Barrie,	91
S. R. Crockett,	96
Ian Maclaren,	100

Friends in Arcady

Charles Dana Gibson,	105
A. B. Frost,	108
F. Marion Crawford,	115
Henry van Dyke,	130

Arcadian Opinions

	PAGE
Summer Reading,	137
Sant' Ilario in Camp,	140
A Legend of the Happy Valley,	144
A Plea for Diana,	148
A Cure for the Malady of Cleverness,	154
The Patriotic Novel,	157

SUPPRESSED CHAPTERS

A NEW DOLLY DIALOGUE

WITH ACKNOWLEDGMENTS TO ANTHONY HOPE, AUTHOR OF "THE PRISONER OF ZENDA," "THE DOLLY DIALOGUES," ETC., ETC.

"IT'S a small world," said Dolly, pouring the tea slowly that I might admire the curve of her wrist.

"But large enough to hold the one woman in the world for me, Lady Mickleham," I ventured, as I turned my back upon her and looked out of the window, while I lighted a cigarette.

"Oh, is *she* the gardener's daughter walking down by the greenhouses?" asked Dolly, with her usual pique.

"At any rate she is a hot-house product," I drawled, "ripened by sunshine, flattery, wealth, and culture."

"Coveted by many, and loved by none!" ventured Dolly.

"Owned by nobody and loved by one," said I, sadly.

Lady Mickleham looked pensively into the bottom of her tea-cup.

"You are only making phrases," at length said Dolly.

"And *that* is better than making love, Lady Mickleham."

"You can't speak with authority," flashed Dolly, "for you always make phrases but never make love!"

"Except to another man's wife," I added, with a glance at Dolly.

"Because it can never commit you to matrimony," she remarked. "You never mean business," she added, spitefully.

"Love is an art and not a trade, Lady Mickleham. Business is for common people."

"Now you are talking like Mr. Hope," snapped Dolly. "I met him the other night at the Dowager's, and all his sentences were built like that."

"He thinks the modern young woman likes that kind," I mused.

"Why?"

"Because it passes for cleverness, Lady Mickleham, and we brutes like to think that you are clever."

"Aren't we, Mr. Brute?"

"You are always cleverer than you seem," I replied, sententiously.

"But Mr. Hope makes us seem cleverer than we are," affirmed Dolly.

"Mr. Hope does not half know *you*," said I, hoping that Dolly might grasp the delicate compliment.

Dolly poured another cup of tea with her left hand, showing another equally beautiful wrist.

"I wonder if Mr. Hope ever met a woman who would listen to a man who spoke in epigrams for five continuous minutes?" I mused as I lighted another cigarette.

"There never was such a man," replied Dolly. "When men talk they orate for ten minutes, and expect the women to listen in rapt attention."

"That's to prevent the women from chattering," said I, with rare courtesy.

"The talk of the advanced young woman of society is not chatter," cut in Dolly.

"It's worse!"

"What?"

"Vulgar," I murmured, with my eyes on Dolly's little curls.

There was silence for the space of half a minute.

"The women in Mr. Hope's stories are not vulgar," at length ventured Dolly.

"Atrociously smart," said I.

"Why can't we say bright things?" queried Dolly.

"You do—but not in modern novels."

"Why?"

"You are simply allowed to ask conundrums for the men to answer in double-headed epigrams," I replied.

"But don't men like to think that they are giving women a lot of superior information?" asked Dolly, glancing out of the corners of her eyes.

"We do like to patronize you," I admitted, in a

moment of rare generosity. "But we also like to love you," I added, pensively.

"Well, and aren't we lovable?" Dolly asked, with a bewitching smile.

"Not in current fiction," I said. "There you are blasé, inquisitive, and immodest," I continued, showing unusual warmth.

"Not all that!" protested Dolly.

"More, much more," said I, walking toward the chimney-place. "Your talk is like the crackling of thorns under a pot, and you hope to enter the kingdom of knowledge by way of the backstairs of impertinent frankness. You wish to make men admire and respect you by talking of subjects that they reserve for their grosser moments."

"Now you are horrid, perfectly horrid, and you may go home," said Dolly, petulantly.

"Would you drive me away from you to the women of those books?" I asked, gently.

"You may stay," said Dolly, as she poured another cup of tea with both wrists.

TRILBY'S CHRISTMAS

IT was on the night of that famous Christmas supper in the place St. Anatole des Arts, when Zouzou and the others had sung their songs and the three policemen were laid out in a stupor behind the stove, that the Laird and Taffy and Trilby and Little Billee had a little conversation (as they sat apart on the model throne eating their plum-pudding) that is not recorded in the book.

"Ay, maun," said the Laird, "but they're making a fuss about us in America!"

"It's all on account of Trilby," said Little Billee, with a fond look at her knuckle-bone teeth.

"They are all palavering a lot of tommy-rot about me," cut in Trilby, speaking in her best English, which she learned from her Irish father, and which was classical, though it smacked of County Cork.

"Worse than that, my dear Trilby," said Taffy, whirling Svengali around his head like an Indian club, between drinks. "Lots of pretty women over there, I am told, are raving over you simply because they think it is 'advanced' and 'up to date' to admire a woman whom they are pleased to think a little bit wicked."

"Me wicked!" shrieked Trilby, her Irish up—"and me the best *blanchisseuse de fin* in the Quartier Latin."

"It isn't the laundry work that attracts their admiration, my lass," said the Laird, in his most fatherly manner. "It's the posing for 'the altogether' and several other little incidents in your career that make you interesting for them."

"Oh," said Trilby, in real distress, "I've been trying for months to forget all those things, and now I am to become a literary classic on account of them!" (Trilby caught the fine language from the lamented O'Ferrall when he was loquacious in his cups.)

"The penalty of fame," said the philosophic Laird, "is to be indiscriminately praised, and generally for the wrong thing. I suppose that I shall be remembered longer for my singing of 'The Laird of Cockpen' than for my Royal Academy pictures."

"Which is right," growled Taffy, who had recently come from Barbizon. "The Royal Academy seldom confers immortality on a worthy painter."

"Those Americans don't seem to love Trilby for the things that make us love her," piped up Little Billee. "They talk and write a great deal about the mere accidental things in her character, but they don't see that we all love her because she is simply a royal, good comrade with no frills about her—with a man's standard of honor, which she keeps to the uttermost."

"Little Billee," cried Trilby, reaching for him with her slipper, "in the language of an American friend of mine, you're a chump!"

"The trouble with Billee," mused Taffy, "is that he is too high strung, and does not take exercise enough. He is just the sort of a fellow who generally 'dies for love' in novels. It isn't nice, and there is no need for it in novels or real life. Five miles a day on a trotting horse will save his life."

"Trilby will save my life," sighed Billee, with a tender glance at her freckles.

"The worst thing I've heard said about our good friend, Du Maurier, who is bound to make us famous," said Taffy, switching away from the sentimental Billee, "is that he writes neither good English nor good French, but a mixture of the slang of each, which thirty years from now will be almost unintelligible without a glossary."

"And yet they call it a revival of the style of Thackeray!" snorted the Laird.

"We must not pick our friends to pieces on Christmas night," said Taffy, rising. "What the story of our old studio is teaching them over in England and America is that there is nothing in this world to be compared to the loyal comradeship of men, and women too, who love each other as brothers, who seize the day of pleasure as it passes, and stand closer together when the night of sorrow comes. Up all of you! Dodor, Gecko, Zouzou—Drink the Christmas toast. Here's to my friend and my brother—all mankind! (*Sings*)

> " Drink, every one;
> Pile up the coals,
> Fill the red bowls,
> Round the old tree!"

NARCISSUS AND HESPER ON WHEELS

WITH ACKNOWLEDGMENTS TO RICHARD LE GALLIENNE, AUTHOR OF "THE BOOK-BILLS OF NARCISSUS."

WHEN Narcissus asked Hesper to go a-wheeling, there had been a great thaw in midwinter that cleared the streets of snow, and then a keen frost that made them all crisp and hard and smooth as any poet and his maid could wish. The sun was shining very bright and the sky was waving its blue over them; the eyes of Hesper were very bright and blue also with the joy of living on such a day. But Narcissus thought it was the light of love in her eyes. Now, as everybody knows, Narcissus is a vain man.

The talk began at the foot of a long hill that overlooks a broad river reaching to the sea. They had chattered before about tires, and high gears, and up-curve handle-bars; but when they reached the foot of the hill and caught the first glimpse of the river that was to broaden and sweep into great majesty as they ascended the hill, they knew that they must talk. For Narcissus thought he was a poet, and Hesper half-believed him.

"It is a very long hill," said Hesper, with her

wistful eyes on the summit, "and I am glad that I am not to take it alone."

"Life is a longer hill," said Narcissus, with a sigh, "and we are taking it alone."

"We don't have to," chirped Hesper, with a dangerous twinkle in her eyes.

"Some of us do," still sighed Narcissus. "We are philosophers."

"The wisest men have always wed," called Hesper, in little trilling catches, as she panted over a hummock in the road.

Then they reached a short level place about halfway up, and Narcissus said that they would stop a while, and he would tell her why! So they leaned across their saddles looking in each other's eyes.

"I've thought it all out," said Narcissus, in his most oracular manner, "and this is Wisdom: Love is no doubt the finest expression of the joy of life. It is not a delusion, but a very real thing while it lasts. But every man who has lived thirty years knows that the joy of life is an affair of youth. It is mind and heart and body all awake to new sensations. Very well," he continued, as though Hesper were agreeing with him, "we know then that for the forty or fifty years that are left us of living we must see and feel the glory fade from the spectacle of the world. Instead of being a spontaneous joy, life is to gradually become a cool, gray monotony of living. At its very best it is that—even without the stings of misfortune that may be added to it."

"Well, what of it?" asked Hesper. "What has that to do with the marriage question?"

"Everything! If a man must not only endure this forty years of growing old for himself, but see the woman he loves and worships going down the same gray walk to death—is he not in a tenfold more tragical plight? And the more he loves her, if he is a man of sensitive feeling, the more he must suffer. It is not a crisis of a day, an accident of fortune to be met and conquered—that is easy; but it is all there is of life—immitigably *all!*"

"And to escape that increased anguish you would voluntarily choose to let the woman you love go her 'gray walk to death' alone?" asked Hesper.

"Surely—that is wisdom for both."

"Oh, you cowardly, selfish man!" she hurled at him, with snapping eyes. "You call love 'the finest expression of the joy of life,' and yet you would miss it for a year-and-a-day, simply that for a score or more of years you may in tranquil loneliness watch the color and sunlight fade from the landscape, with no woman to bother you about her own views of the spectacle. You are the final product of luxurious sophistry. You don't deserve this one hour of sunshine and glorious exercise, let alone the view of the river yonder. You can't always have these things either, and yet you seize and enjoy them when you may! Why not love also? Give me a year of perfect companionship with the man I love, and the rest of life may be as gray as it pleases fate to send it.

For *me* it will always glow with the memory of that year!"

Hesper was on fire with anger, and she left him and wheeled furiously up the hill.

Now Narcissus was a strong man, as well as vain and selfish, and within a few yards he overtook her fleeing and struggling on a steep place. He reached one hand to her saddle, and so gently pushed her over the steep place and up to the summit, that, when they stood in an embrasure of the wall at the top and looked out at the glorious river, she had already half forgiven him.

"It was good of you to do that after I had said angry words to you," she said.

"Oh, I have a great deal of strength to spare," said Narcissus, vainly.

"Don't you think you might have enough strength to spare for the woman you really loved to last you for the rest of your life?" laughed Hesper in his very face. Then she whirled away down the steep hill like a swallow dipping to the level of the river.

And whether Narcissus ever overtook her to answer the question, I know not.

LITTLE WAYOFF

WITH ACKNOWLEDGMENTS TO HENRIK IBSEN, AUTHOR OF
"LITTLE EYOLF," "A DOLL'S HOUSE," ETC.

SCENE—*A summer-house overlooking a Norwegian Fjord.* ALLMERS *and his wife* RITA *seated within, looking out to sea, and earnestly conversing.*

ALLMERS: You must realize once for all, Rita, that I am seriously afflicted with the disease of the decade—Ibsenism—and you must conform your life to that new condition.

RITA: Yes, yes—I'll try, dear. What is this awful malady?

ALLMERS: Ibsenism is the yellow jaundice of the soul.

RITA: Horrors! Is there no remedy suggested in all the books of your great library?

ALLMERS (*solemnly*): None. The peculiarity of the disease is that no one who catches it wants to be cured.

RITA: What! Are you content to live the rest of your life seeing things sicklied o'er with a yellow-green light?

ALLMERS: Not only content but glad to do it!

The intellect demands this sacrifice of the man who is truly wise.

RITA: But I am naturally of a hopeful disposition. I love sunshine and joy and good-fellowship. True, I am temporarily depressed by the drowning of our only son, Little Wayoff, but I think that in time I might begin to smile again if you would only love me as you used.

ALLMERS (*impressively*): Love is the temporary insanity of the emotions! I am sane.

RITA: But once you loved me passionately, and we were very happy.

ALLMERS: Yes, yes—happiness is the final expression of insanity. The truly healthy man is never happy.

RITA (*with resignation*): Well, then, I'll try hard to be miserable enough to be a congenial companion for you. Only tell me the way.

ALLMERS: First of all you must rake through the records of the past for all the diseases, crimes, and terrible weaknesses of your ancestors. When you have discovered them, carefully ponder over them, for by the immutable Laws of Nature you have inherited them all and carry them around in your beautiful body. They are liable to break out at any time, singly or all together.

RITA (*frightened to death*): Save me, save me dear! Am I truly only a mausoleum for the dead past of my family?

ALLMERS (*sternly*): You are all that and more too.

Nature always adds a few frills to inherited weakness and crime on her own account. By the law of the universe you ought to be a little worse than any of your ancestors.

RITA (*in despair*): That settles it! I don't want to live any longer. Throw me in the fjord yonder to help feed the pretty fishes along with Little Wayoff. Oh, my boy, my boy, your mother comes to you! (*Rushes toward the edge of the cliff.*)

ALLMERS (*catching her*): Stay! Do you really want to die?

RITA: Yes, believe me, yes! Who could live in such a world as this!

ALLMERS (*with a gleam of pleasure in his eyes*): Come to my arms, my own love! Now, at last, are you my true soul-mate. Under the shadow of this awful gloom we can go through the world together, doing our little best to thicken the sorrow and despair wherever we find it. This is our destiny. Come. (*Embraces her.*)

RITA: And after thirty or forty years of this gloom we may be fitted to join our beloved Little Wayoff in another world?

ALLMERS: Perhaps, perhaps!

[CURTAIN.]

LOST CHORDS

WITH ACKNOWLEDGMENTS TO GEORGE EGERTON, AUTHOR OF "DISCORDS."

SHE sits on a fallen log by the banks of a tumbling mountain brook; the air is filled with the odor of fir, and the glint of sunshine is on the moss, and in her gray eyes, and upon her bronze-gold hair. This unequalled combination of moss and sunshine and feminine loveliness is enough to stir to its depths the heart of any man. How much more the heart of the impressionable poet at her feet!

"You see in me," she said to him, in her trumpet-voice, "the embodiment of the new idea of womanhood. Once my life was nearly wrecked by 'ignorant innocence.' I've risen to my present serene altitude by a thorough course of 'all-seeing knowledge.' When I say *knowledge* you must understand that I refer to all the evil and wickedness in which men are habitually engaged. A three-years' course in the study of vice has, it is true, disillusionized me —but it has made me strong!"

As she said this she tossed a bowlder into the tumbling stream with her left hand, then placidly brushed the dust from her great fingers with one of the ribbons of her very simple, but perfectly correct, Paris-made gown.

"Tell me," asked the poet, with beseeching eyes, "what are all these vicious things that I must understand before I can be strong? Pity my ignorance. You know that I have been five years at Eton, where I was captain of our football team, and four years at Oxford, where I was stroke of the 'Varsity crew—but what I know is nothing when compared to you. Vice and wickedness are neither required nor elective at Oxford. Please pity me! You know that I have no sister to warn me of the cruel and wicked world."

"Poor fellow!" she replied, softening her voice to the mellow tones of thunder. "How many promising young men are lost because they have no sisters to warn them of the sinfulness of the great world! I'll be a sister to you, my dear boy."

Saved! murmured the brook, as it tumbled along into the valley. *Saved!* And the wind in the firs caught up the melody and added to it—Saved, for she knows it all!

The poet ventured near enough to kiss the hem of her Paris gown. Then in a kind, sisterly way she told him of all the outrageously wicked things she had discovered during her period of regeneration.

"But, oh, my dear sister," said the poet, blushing from head to foot all over his puny six-feet-two of manly strength, "must I do all these wicked things before I can be considered strong enough to battle with the world?"

She looked unutterable things at him with her great eyes, and slowly said: "Know you not that it is only for a few of the great, soulful spirits of the world to *do* these things! But for most women and all men it is enough for their regeneration that they simply *read* about them thoroughly, and, if they have the talent, write books about them for innocent boys and girls to read by the sweet and gentle fireside of home."

"But don't you think their mothers might object to their reading such books?" ventured the poet, doubtfully.

"Mothers!" she shrieked, scornfully. "Don't speak to me of mothers! Oh, the crimes of ignorance that are committed in their name! Mothers are women who habitually associate with Men—think of it, great, gross, wicked Men—who actually pay their rent and buy household supplies for them, and feed and clothe their children; yea, and even send them to school and college. Think of a woman who will accept these favors from a man, and then talk to me of mothers! My boy, my boy, how far you are from the kingdom of the new womanhood! Go, I cannot talk to you more now. Some day, if you return to me scarred with crime, I may venture again to associate with you. But not now—you contaminate me with your presence. Go!"

The poet kissed the hem of her garment again, and vanished amid the trees.

"BUY THE IDIOT BRAND"

WITH ACKNOWLEDGMENTS TO JOHN KENDRICK BANGS, AUTHOR OF "COFFEE AND REPARTEE," "THE IDIOT," ETC.

"WE'RE going to start a great Consolidated American Humor Factory," said the Idiot, as he caromed on a buckwheat-cake and hit the sausage square. This off-hand remark immediately gained the attention of Mrs. Pedagog's breakfast-table.

"Who are we?" asked the Bibliomaniac with his usual undercurrent of scepticism.

"Bangs and I," said the Idiot, as he pocketed buckwheat-cake No. 1, and drew No. 2 into fine position.

"What Bangs? John Kendrick Bangs, the humorist?" asked the Poet, in wide-eyed astonishment. "Do you know a real live author?"

"The same," said the Idiot, playing for position on the left rail of his plate. "Bangs and I are bosom friends. You must understand that John Kendrick Bangs who writes for the great magazines, J. K. Bangs of the Sunday papers, Carlyle Smith of the comic weeklies, J. Kendrick Bangs of the Yonkers *Citizen*, and John K. Bangs the politician, are one and the same individual. I am the bosom friend of the whole aggregation."

"The aggregation must be shy of bosom friends when it takes you," sniffed Mr. Pedagog.

"Wrong again, as usual, Mr. Pedagog," chirped the Idiot as he reached for the maple syrup and dug the old gentleman in the ribs. "I'm a very profitable friend and Bangs knows a good thing when he sees it. That's why I am in on the ground floor of the Consolidated American Humor Factory. Great idea, great head, great man!"

"Doubt it," grunted the School-master. "Your adjectives are always ten sizes too large for your ideas."

"But you must notice, my charitable friend, that I am gradually growing up to my adjectives," insinuatingly said the Idiot. "Another great idea of mine—start with big adjectives and try hard to live up to them. Before you know it you're a big man. See!"

"That has nothing to do with the Factory. Tell us about it," said Mr. Brief, impatiently.

"Same general line of thought, Mr. Brief," replied the Idiot. "Bangs is nothing if not original. He said to himself one day, 'Here are a lot of fellows I know travelling all over the world for literary and artistic experiences—Material they call it. What's the matter with manufacturing experiences right here at home for half the cost! I believe in encouraging home industries.' So he decided to blow in some money and run for Mayor of Yonkers. That town narrowly missed having a dandy Mayor, but Bangs got his money's worth of experience—and the result was 'Three Weeks in Politics,' one of his most successful books."

"But what about the Factory?" asked the indignant boarders in chorus, looking at the dining-room clock.

"I've just given you the germinal idea," said the Idiot. "Says Bangs to me—'Idiot, old boy, we'll go right ahead manufacturing humorous experiences on a large scale. I'll build a magnificent villa on the banks of the Hudson, not far from my home. It shall be divided into about fifty suites of comfortable apartments, with good table-board, plenty of outdoor sports, and everything to keep the guests in good humor. I'll invite up for long visits a choice assortment of mothers-in-law, bad boys, Irish comedians, Yankee farmers, summer girls, brakemen, bunco-steerers, and all the other indispensable characters for American humor. Then I'll just come over for an hour or two every day and visit with them —and my books will write themselves. And you shall have a ground-floor suite, Mr. Idiot, and manage the whole show. Are you with me?' 'I'm yours for life, Mr. Bangs,' said I. No humor from this Factory genuine unless countersigned by me. *Buy the Idiot Brand!*"

"And so, Mrs. Pedagog," said the Idiot, turning to the head of the table, "I give you notice that I must quit your hospitable board. But I'll invite you all up to stay awhile at the Factory. Bangs needs you in his business. Ta, ta!"

SOME REMARKS OF MAJOR BRACE

APROPOS OF "WINDFALLS OF OBSERVATION," BY EDWARD S. MARTIN.

"I'VE been having a delightful afternoon," said Major Brace, as he slid into his favorite corner of the Club café, and rang the bell. The younger men were dropping in from down-town with the worriment of a financial crisis written on their faces, but the Major's serenity was perennial and contagious. They liked to hear him talk, and this was his favorite hour. As the Martini was placed before him he continued: "While you youngsters have been hustling down town for dollars that are not in circulation, I have been up in the Club library reading Martin's book, 'Windfalls of Observation.' There's a wise youth for you! He has a good, workable philosophy which contains my three cardinal virtues for the man of the world — Courage, Gumption, Serenity."

"Come, now, Major," said the Impertinent Youth. "Everybody knows that you pat Martin on the back because he occasionally puts your harangues in print. A little bit flattered, eh?"

"There is something in what you say," replied the Major, affably. "We all have our little vanities. But discounting the vanity, I want you boys to read the 'Windfalls.' I am twice the age of any one of you, and I know what is good for a man of thirty. And I say that it *is* good for men of your years to believe many of the things that Martin talks about. Most of you are university and professional men. You imagine that you have lived a long time, and that you see clear through to the end of the journey. As a matter of fact you are just fairly started. You are all a little cynical; it takes the form of mistrust of all men and most women. When you only knew your own folks and a limited circle of friends, you imagined that the world was filled with good, decent people. But your business and professions have brought you in violent contact with the *other* kind, and now you go to the other extreme and believe that most men are rogues. Oh, the cruelty of the wisdom of youth!

"But what I like in these essays of Martin's is the fine charity which seasons the wisdom of youth. He looks on the world with the keen eyes of a young man, but tempers his judgments with that equipoise and good-will which we are accustomed to associate with a lovable old age. That is why I am commending his philosophy to you. The sooner you put yourself in that attitude, the sooner will you grasp the secret of the perpetual youth of the heart. When you begin to look for the finer, honest side in the men and women you meet, you yourself become the touchstone that reveals it in them. You find your way in life cheered with this atmosphere of good-will, which you in part create yourself, and partly reveal in others.

"I know I am preaching a little," said the Major, as he noticed signs of uneasiness among the boys. "But that is one of the privileges of my years. Besides you owe me something for listening to your long debates on legal and commercial questions, that are of no earthly account to anybody but money-grubbers. I am in dead earnest about this, because I like the enthusiasms of youth and hate its cynicisms; and when I find a young man writing sweet-tempered, acute, serene, and manly essays like these, I want other young men to read them. They are so utterly without pretence or affectation of knowledge, and the humor ripples through the pages like a clear brook in a meadow.

"You must not think from what I have been saying that he has no eye for human frailties. Why, the satire pricks something at every turn, like briers along the brook! But it is the peaceful dwelling together in these pages of satire and good feeling, humor and good manners, that makes the charm of the book for me.

"Now, you must not tell Martin what I have been saying. He'll think I want him to publish some more of my Views. I don't. Waiter, take the orders!"

ARCADIAN LETTERS

TO TERENCE MULVANEY

APROPOS OF "MANY INVENTIONS," BY RUDYARD KIPLING.

AH, Terence, my boy, Mr. Kipling has been telling us some more of your stories, and they are making glad the hearts of your old friends. We had heard that you were out of the army, and boss of a gang of coolies on a railway in Central India—"Ker'nel on the railway line, an' a consequinshal man," as you graphically put it; and we feared your new job would put an end to your tales. But here you are again in finer form than ever! For myself, I don't think you ever span a better yarn than "My Lord, the Elephant"—though there are impertinent fellows who assert that you have often come nearer the truth. They don't know you, my boy, and I want to say that I have no more doubt that you rode the *must* elephant around the barracks at Cawnpore, than I have that *Dinah Shadd* is the best wife that ever fell to the lot of one of the Queen's soldiers. And that other tale of yours about the man you nicknamed "Love-o'-Women"—I wonder if you know that it is what literary men call "a pathetic tragedy?" No, you don't, Terence, and I hope you never may—for when you begin to look on your stories in *that* fashion they'll cease to be worth telling. What people like about you over on this side of the earth is that you, and *Jock* and *Ortheris* as well, are brave men who take hold of the things nearest you without much bellowing; and you never whine when you are hurt. As *Ortheris* puts it, "I ain't a recruity to go whinin' about my rights to this an' my rights to that, as if I couldn't look after myself. My rights! 'Streweth A'mighty! I'm a man!"

I don't mind telling you, confidentially, that we need some tales like yours and Mr. Kipling's over here. We have a good many fine young men writing stories, but they spend most of their time putting frills on them. As *Stanley* would say, there are "a lot o' bloomin' petticoats" in their stories, and they sit around on "piazzas" and talk to young men who are about as useless as a subaltern just out from England. Nobody ever does anything; they simply think great big thoughts that congest in their bloomin' heads.

You are away off in India, and might think from this that we are a rum lot—but we are not. We have plenty of men who can do things without making a fuss—fight great battles, build immense railroads, invent wonderful machines, or put a World's Fair together in two years that beat all records. Mr. Kipling does not like us because we are too sensitive about many other things that we can't do; and that's true, too. But then, you know, we should not get ahead if we were not a little sensitive. You don't know where to stretch a shoe until it pinches you.

But it does not matter what Mr. Kipling thinks of us; we know a good story when we see it, and we shall go right along reading his and yours, and asking for more, and waiting for that Great Novel which you and I know he is man enough to write some day.

With my regards to *Dinah Shadd*.

TO EVADNE GALBRAITH

APROPOS OF "THE HEAVENLY TWINS," BY MADAM SARAH GRAND.

DEAR MADAM: As the heroine of a book about which England has been talking, you have, no doubt, by this time gauged English opinion in regard to your advanced views about the rights of women. But the American view must be rather vague to you by reason of your aloofness from our sympathies in such questions. I know that, with your strong wish to look on Truth squarely, you will pardon a very explicit statement of the causes which have operated to keep American women out of accord with your views as interpreted by Madam Grand in "The Heavenly Twins." I think that your friend *Mrs. Malcomson* expressed very tersely this feeling of "difference" when she said, with some indignation: "Oh, yes, we have our reward, we Englishwomen. We religiously obey our men. We do nothing of which they disapprove. We are the meekest sheep in the world. We scorn your independent, outspoken American women; we think them bold and unwomanly, and do all we can to be as unlike them as possible. And what happens?

Do our men adore us? Well, they continue to say so. But it is the Americans they marry."

If you will pardon a blunt statement of it, I think you will find that it is this very "difference" which will incline the American girl to be amused at your warmth about certain rights for women, rather than be stirred up to join you in a crusade for them. She will toss her pretty head and say, with accustomed frankness:

"Bless you, dear Madam, why should we organize to make a fight for these rights, when we have them already without the asking! Of course American girls do marry the kind of wicked men whom you preach against—and very often they are Englishmen. But then, you know, we don't do it from ignorance or because we have been educated in a corral. Dear no! We either find the men interesting, or they have a title or some position that we want to share with them. Our eyes are open, and we know what we want, and generally get it. Sometimes we find that we have made a bad bargain. Of course, that is a part of the risk of the game. But if we do, we follow the example of our American fathers when they have been caught by a bad bargain—we speculate in futures in the hope of making things come out even. Few American girls stake all their life on love and marriage; we can play the game for so many other stakes. There is social position for one; reputation as an intellectual woman for another (dear me, how easily we can make the men believe that we are learned); then there are the Church and organized charity which give us abundant outlets for our executive energies. For you must realize that we *are* executive above all things. That is why we are ceasing to be morbid. And, my dear lady, I fear you are very morbid. You yourself have said that thought which does not lead to action makes one morbid, and that has been your trouble. If you had simply spent two or three months *organizing* your crusade, you would have forgotten all your trouble. It would not matter whether you accomplished anything or not; the cure is in the very act of organization. Why, we have doctors who will tell you on the sly that they have encouraged the organizing mania among women as a cure for nervous prostration. I know of one particularly bad case where the physician hinted to the patient that there was a crying need for a society to provide East-Side waifs with tops in season. It was harmless, and it cured her. (That is the beauty of our men by the way, they let us do as we please, and yet manage us.)"

The American girl, with her usual audacity, has filled most of my letter. But I want to say a word for the American man in contrast to the men in your story. Your men don't seem to have enough to do —that is why, perhaps, they spend so much time deceiving women. (I am referring to your men as *you* see them, and not as I believe they are.) Now the American man is a busy creature. If he does not have to work for a living, he is apt to create some engrossing work for his mere good pleasure.   After all that has been said about it, we really have very few idle rich men here ; there are a great many more idle " little brothers of the rich "—a class of parasites who would be idle in any condition of life.   When our men *are* busy, they are in it heart and soul for success, and that leaves little time for what is vicious. The spare time the American man has is occupied by some bright girl, who probably " knows the world " as well as he does and often "gives him points." You must not think them " bold and unwomanly," as your friend says.   They simply look at things with clear eyes, and with a heart filled with that goodwill for men and women that " thinketh no evil "— but, nevertheless, *sees* it if it exists.

That, I take it, is all that you would ask or seek by your crusade.   Just cross the ocean and find it !

Kindly express my thanks to *Diavolo* and *Angelica*, the heavenly twins, for the rich amusement their amazing personal cleverness has afforded us.

TO DIANA OF THE CROSSWAYS, SURREY

APROPOS OF "LOVE-LETTERS OF A WORLDLY WOMAN," BY
MRS. W. K. CLIFFORD.

DEAR DIANA: You are always a graceful woman, in important and in trivial things, and in nothing are you so often tactful as in your little remembrances for days and seasons. You write me that the hedges and the Downs in Surrey are full of the perfume of Spring, and you feel sure that I shall be wandering into the country very soon to breathe the odor of apple-blossoms. So you send me the "Love-Letters of a Worldly Woman," which will be just the little book I want to read on the way down to the country, in the cars, and think about on the way back. "You will go a-looking for your lost youth in the springtime, and this little book will show you how far away it is," you add with a touch of irony.

The letter and the book came as I was starting for Arcady and the old college, and I have read it while skimming along green fields, or sitting under the elms. It has brought back the old mood, as you knew it would, and I am not sure as I sit here whether it was yesterday or a hundred years ago, that I left these gray old cloisters and closed the doors on this world of sentiment and aspiration. For it is to this world that these letters belong.

The title, as you must have felt, is a misnomer—for none of these are the letters of a "worldly woman." In the three parts of the book it is essentially the same woman who writes—at different ages and degrees of experience. But she is always the woman of sentiment, romance, and aspiration—the sort of woman whom the group of "digs" in cap and gown, who are discussing the "eternal verities" in the next room, would worship, and then write perfectly correct hexameters in her honor. They would believe that her little affectations of cynicism were real worldly wisdom, and stand a little bit in awe of them. But you, Diana, who knew the real world and suffered in it before you married dear old Redworth, would never be deceived by these assertions of womanly independence.

I know what you think about her and I can almost hear you say it: "This woman is lovable, but she would be very uncomfortable in a family; I know, for I was once like her; and if I had married Tom in those days I should have ruined his career, simply by continually urging him to make what I called 'sacrifices' for success. That dear man is now a type of the right kind of success, but there is none of that sort of heroism in it which the woman who writes these letters worships in a man."

What you and I really like about her is a certain fervor and intensity of love which she lavishes on her ideal man. You know there never was such a man (except Tom Redworth), but if she should find him some day she would be sorry that she ever married *Sir Noel*, even though he should be Prime Minister. It is the possibility that a woman may cherish such a delusion about him that makes a man love her. If he can only be the hook on which she hangs her ideal man, he is content. So long as she does not distinguish between the hook and the ideal, the real man is happy; but when she attempts to differentiate them his trouble begins. That is why you and I think that the woman of these clever stories is lovable, but uncomfortable.

What I most like about her is that she clearly distinguishes between what is really interesting and what is simply conventional, what is respectable and what is important. That is a line which few women draw, and not a host of men. I am inclined to think that it is as important as the " moral law "—perhaps it *is* the moral law in a nutshell.

But it is growing very late; the college clock is striking, and there is a rumpus outside the door. It is the boy (who calls me " Uncle " when he wants to tease, and " Jack " when he wants what he is pleased to call a *loan*) who enters with his comrades. " It is almost time for the Owl train back to the city, old man," he says, " and I am sorry you can't stay for our spread." The boys all carry mysterious packages, and I have a suspicion that there is little left of the " loan " the boy negotiated a few hours ago.

It is a cheap price for a happy day and an evening of pleasant reverie in the very room that was once mine; nothing left of the original shell but this old table which the boy says "must have come out of the Ark." At any rate I know that Noah was young when he bought it, and he wrote reams of letters on it to a woman who before the flood was called Diana Antonia Merion.

THE CLOISTERS, COLLEGE OF ARCADY.

TO ONE WHO IS TIRED OF READING

DEAR BOY: You write me from your lovely Southern island that you are sitting in the sun, and looking down a long avenue of live-oaks, festooned with hanging moss and mistletoe. From your piazza you can see the deer dart across the open space, and hear the whir of partridge wings when they are startled. Over all the animated stillness lingers the low music of the summer ocean. And yet you are discontented because your books have lost their charm, and even dear old Horatius Flaccus, who is your solace and your cheer, has ceased to charm you. And you expect me (shivering by a radiator, and listening to the sleet biting at the window glass) to sympathize with you! For long years we have been friends together, but my friendship does not reach that far.

I could never understand why a man of your years and philosophy should make your appetite for reading a test of your general health. I suspect that it is because you have been always a successful man of affairs, and books have been your recreation. When you don't enjoy your recreation you rightly infer that your vitality is running a little low. It would be equally true of horseback riding, or whist playing if they chanced to be your favorite amusements—and yet who would let his conscience worry him about loss of enjoyment in them!

You have the appreciative amateur's over-esteem for books and book-making. I have never heard you express any admiration for the work of great iron and steel contractors; that happens to be your occupation, and you know how it is done, and what success in it costs. I have seen you come home after an all-day wrestle with giants in the railway world, whom you have brought 'round to your way of thinking at a directors' meeting. It cost you blood and brains, and yet you showed no elation, no sense of victory; you simply poked sarcasm at the whole lot of them, whom you had barely beaten, and, most of all, at yourself for expending so much energy on the affair.

Then you would have your dinner, and your pipe, and the newest book perhaps, or a very old one. At intervals you would break out into explosions of admiration for some deftly turned phrase, or rhythmic line which a youngster somewhere on this or the other side of the sea had reeled off because he had spent most of his life in an easy-chair and liked to fool with pen and paper and his own emotions.

If you had ever come nearer to it than the printed page, you would have a clear idea of what "an old woman's work" this writing business often is. It would be a rare sight to see a great, strong, alert giant like you pinned down to a desk, playing with words as though they were blocks in a puzzle. I can imagine you, after an hour or two of it, rising in your wrath and turning the whole business over to your type-writer, as suited better to her placid, mechanical way of life.

"Give me men," you would cry, "to move my way, and carry out my ideas! Let me deal with real forces and great masses of material things that may be builded into realizations of my wildest dreams! I want to live, while I live, down to my finger-tips. This playing with a dictionary isn't living."

And yet you are sitting there in the balmy South growling because you now prefer to look down the avenue of live-oaks rather than read a book! You don't realize how perfectly sane and healthy you now are, and that you don't want to read because your tired nerves are adjusting themselves to a normal way of life, and to the gentle healing of Nature. Don't come to me for sympathy; but go out and kill a deer.

TO JEAN AT TWENTY-TWO

AFTER long silence, dear Jean, you write to your "venerable friend," and ask whether among your New-Year resolves you shall include a prohibition of all fiction. "At twenty-two," you say, "I begin to see that I have been living in a Fool's Paradise, and I am not quite sure that I have not built the greater part of it with novels. If my mental furniture is only a useless lot of illusions, I want to get rid of it as soon as possible. If novels are only fairy tales for grown-up boys and girls, why should a sensible woman waste time over them? You have lived thirty years longer than I, and your friends call you happy. Come, be frank with me!"

I can remember very well, Jean, when I felt just as old, restless, and unsatisfied as you do now, and it was about thirty years ago. Since then I think I have grown a little younger every year, until I have become a gray-haired and rotund youth, with a fondness for chimney-corners and long pipes and after-dinner naps—and novels. I'll confess this early, so that you may realize what a mistake you make in asking my advice.

People of a certain age know that until a boy gets well into the twenties the most interesting thing in the world to him is himself. If he falls in love during that period, it is only a kind of huge *fête* to his own vanity. He reads fiction to find in it the reflection and glorification of his own qualities. But before twenty-five he wakens to a knowledge of his Fool's Paradise. Then ensues a most unhappy period, when he is deeply disgusted with himself and everybody else—for, conscious of his own absurdity, as a last sop to his egotism, he persuades himself that all the world is equally foolish. That is the period of pessimism, doubt, heroic resolve, and small accomplishment.

But one day, ever to be remembered, a little rift appears in the clouds, and he sees how fair a world the sun is shining upon, and how interesting are the people in it. Before he knows it, he is absorbed in watching the glorious and pathetic pageant of life, and sings with a modern poet:

> "Easier may I tolerate
> My neighbor than myself not hate."

The more absorbed he becomes in others the less he thinks of himself; he has discovered the fountain of contentment, and drunk of the waters of perpetual youth. This is his last illusion. Men have wrapped themselves in it, and at the end of fourscore years have lain down to rest in it, with their hearts full of gentle thoughts and a great hope, and their memory gladdened with good deeds.

You are laughing, no doubt, at my sermon, but it is the privilege of elderly men to preach. "Yes," you say, "but what has it all to do with my question about novels?" Well, I confess that I like to come around to a text by way of a lot of platitudes, especially when I have a listener so patient and so fair as you. Do you not see that, if life is the most engaging study and the chiefest consolation for the living, the best novels, which are the work of men profoundly interested in life, are a force that makes for happiness?

Your opportunities and mine for seeing much of this fascinating show may be sadly limited by health or circumstance; perhaps we have such a part to play in the ranks that we march wearily along in a treadmill way, and only see the faces in our own battalion. But, in the little halts for rest by the way, around the camp-fire, tired though we be, we may read the reports of our more fortunate comrades who have had a place on the reviewing-stand. How it kindles our imagination and warms the cockles of our hearts to feel that we are a part of the great and onward-moving pageant! We have more respect for the men next to us in the ranks after this outlook on the larger life.

So it has happened that the great novelists were men of broad sympathy and tolerance, because they were ennobled by what their faculty of perception revealed to them.

TO A CERTAIN CRITIC

DEAR DROCH: For ten years you have been talking at people about books, and nobody ever has a chance to talk back. I don't think it is quite fair, and that is why I am writing this letter. It will free my mind, though I don't believe you will be square enough to print it.

You must be a rather old man by this time, for you have so little comprehension of the tastes of youth. You seem to think that we take our reading seriously; that we want to think about a book after we have closed its covers; that we are wildly anxious to get at its merits of construction, style, and even morality. Bless your gray hairs, how did you get the idea that the modern youth takes anything seriously, least of all his reading? We have too many amusing things to occupy our time to dwell on any one of them long enough for what our fathers used to call "reflection." Don't you honestly believe that what they thought was "reflection" was simply the ordinary kind of "mooning" which afflicts lazy people? What good ever came of it? So far as I can discover it led to absurdly sensitive consciences which made them all miserable. Then began the habit of "exacting" all kinds of duties from themselves, and their neighbors. The wisest of them began on their neighbors and spent the little time left on themselves. When they ran out of live material for dissection, they fell back on "discussing books"—and I fancy it was in your manner.

I am glad I did not live in those days. Aren't you just a little sorry for yourself sometimes?

But I want to tell you frankly what a book and reading really mean to the modern youth.

We are told on the highest scientific authority that we are "very highly developed organisms." We are complicated and delicately adjusted machines. These machines, under modern conditions, are run on a fuel which we call "excitement." You know what a rattle and jarring takes place in a big threshing-machine when they stop feeding it sheaves of grain? The wise farmer always runs a little straw through while the machine is slowing down to save the wear and tear.

Well, we read books on the same principle exactly. They are the straw that slows down the machine easily when active pleasure and excitement are not at hand. Chaff is just as good as wheat-in-the-sheaf for that purpose.

There is another way of looking at it. You know that modern science has robbed us of our illusions —from babyhood up to maturity. If you never brought yourself up without illusions you can't imagine how dreary it sometimes is. I did not mean to tell you about this—but sometimes the cold, gray light in which we see everything is simply heartbreaking. Perhaps it is only the nervous reaction when the machine is slowing down. It is not so many years ago that I went to sleep crying because all my dolls were so painfully like real people. It was about that time that I first found out that a book was a very good substitute for lost illusions, and I have been taking the medicine ever since. And you critics try your best to rob us of that last refuge for our illusions, by picking it to pieces. Don't, please don't! Yours Reproachfully,

JEAN.

TO A FRIEND STARTING ON A VACATION

MY DEAR JACK: You write that you have the prospect of closing your desk in the office of the *Daily Whirl* for a month, of sweeping the scraps and shreds of Associated Press despatches into your basket, of writing one more "display head" on a "Terrible Loss of Life"—and then for the Wilderness. For weeks you have dreamed of a bed of spruce boughs, of a bark camp with a leaping fire on the side that is open toward the lake—and now you are ready to make it all something better than "a vision of the night." You recall that I once went into camp on Cedar Island, and you would like to know more about the place.

My dear fellow, I envy you the prospect of these weeks in the Adirondacks, and, if I can help you to find the road to the Mysterious Island, I shall surely add to your happiness.

I shall let you find your way to Utica and Boonville by prosaic steam-cars and time-tables.

While you are waiting for dinner at Moose River you will hear strange tales of the horrors of the Old Forge road, in the days before the railroad. Nothing that an Adirondack guide can invent will quite equal the roughness of that road. After five years it is as vividly before me as a memory of yesterday. Yet for out-and-out amusement the "railroad" beats it. You cross a bridge at Moose River, and on the banks of the stream are the "terminal facilities"—a shed containing the entire rolling-stock of the road—a Tom Thumb engine, a short platform car (for passengers) with a zinc roof supported by iron pipes, and another truck for freight and baggage.* After several false starts, which are made without sufficient headway for the first grade, you are off on the strangest piece of railway construction you have ever seen. A pathway has been cut through the densest forest, and the trees on each side are so tall and straight that you seem to be at the bottom of a green canyon. The road-bed is partly graded with logs piled up in squares like a corn-cob house. The rails are wooden scantling, about three by four inches, laid upon parallel unhewn logs. Like two huge brown snakes they creep through the forest, following the sinuosities of the land, and all its little hills and valleys, so that the journey is like a series of toboggan slides. You stop in the heart of the forest, and are invited by the genial old boy (who is conductor, engineer, and fireman, all in one) to help carry wood for the engine. You slide and roll over another hill or two, and then stop at a trout-brook while the engine takes up water through a huge proboscis. By and by,

* Written before the present trunk line was built.

after two hours of adventure, during which you have penetrated nine miles of wilderness, you come upon a winding stream, known as the North Branch.

There is awaiting you a boat which is as strange a craft as any that ever steamed away to a Mysterious Island—flat bottom, square ends, rounded corners, a deck around the smoke-stack, side-wheels driven by levers like grasshopper legs, and a fireman whose chief duty it is to shove the boat around the ox-bows with a pole.

And what a voyage you have up the North Branch in the late afternoon! You are ascending another canyon of green; alders fringe the banks of the stream and dip into it, while above them rise walls of spruce and balsam and hemlock and birch — tier upon tier of variegated green. The river turns on itself like a chain of S's, sometimes almost making a figure 8. You reach the end of the journey up the enchanted stream about supper-time, and are driven in a carryall to the Forge House. From its piazza you get a view of the first of the series of lakes and ponds known as the Fulton Chain, and right at your feet you see a graceful little steamer waiting to carry you to the island.

In the early twilight Captain Jack takes his place at the bow—tall and straight, clear blue eyes, curly iron-gray hair, a trim uniform—altogether the handsomest man on the Chain, as he surely has been one of the best guides for many years. He stands at the wheel, with curious little mail-pouches all around him.

The steamer zigzags from camp to camp, and at every wharf there are men and women with greetings and chaff for Jack. You seem to steam up the lakes between cross-fires of laughter—and now the spirit of the woods is upon you, and you feel that here is freedom, rest, and good-will.

It is dark now, and the camp-fires are twinkling all along the shores. In the tortuous inlets between the lakes you have plucked water-lilies, and raised your eyes to find yourself suddenly out of the darkness on a broad sheet of water that mirrors every star. You glide among the stars, on and on in the keen night-air, until in the very midst of the lake you see a black mound with lights flitting over it. As you near it a voice back of a swinging lantern cries " Hello, Captain Jack," and in a minute your boat scrapes the wharfs of the Mysterious Island.

I need not tell you what you will find there—except that it will be a hearty welcome, a spring-bed in a bark cottage within a few feet of the lake, a number of good guides, a raging hunger, and health and happiness from day to day.

Good-speed to you, and a safe return.

NOVELS THAT EVERYBODY READ

"LORD ORMONT AND HIS AMINTA"

THE women in the novels of George Meredith are so fascinating that beside them real women sometimes seem to be the phantoms of the imagination. He makes them charm you always by their union of feminine qualities with a certain strength at a crisis. Almost without exception the women in Meredith's novels *think*, and occasionally act on reason. But the sign of their womanliness is that at the last they follow the lead of a dominant passion. That is why men are fascinated by them.

The heroine in his romance of "Lord Ormont and his Aminta" adds another striking portrait to his gallery of fair women. *Aminta* is not the speaker of epigrams, as so many of his great characters are; in this novel that *rôle* is reserved for *Lady Charlotte*, a truly wonderful study of an elderly woman of strong intellect and persistent, vital affections. But *Aminta* permeates this story with her beauty, her physical poise, her clear-sightedness in a great moral crisis. She is a woman who rebels against the false position in which she is placed, without indulging in hysterics or heroics. That is unusual in either fiction or life.

There is a dignity about her rebellion, such as characterizes a strong man when he is making up his mind; he does not show his opponent the processes by which he is reaching a conclusion.

The situation developed in the closing chapters of the novel is one of unusual complexity. How can any one justify a beautiful, true woman in leaving so fine a type of man as *Lord Ormont*—"a chivalrous gentleman up to the bounds of his intelligence!" The justification is found in what is fundamental in all Meredith's novels—the very root of his strength and his optimism. From *Feverel* to *Ormont* he has never ceased to show the divine right of every man and woman to seize the one great chance of emotional, mental, and spiritual growth that comes of the perfect companionship of a man and woman who love each other with all their strength. We are all in the hands of a great power which Meredith calls Nature, working by laws which at best we can only imperfectly comprehend. But one thing we can do—and that is follow the dictates of Nature, the great primal impulse that forces us on to the best that is in us unless we thwart it. Meredith always shows the inevitable consequences of thus going against "the laws which men have made for their own convenience." He is not an Anarchist; he believes in law, but he also believes in the right of real strength and integrity to choose out its own path, even if it goes at cross-purposes to the law. Whether one accepts his philosophy or not, one cannot fail to note how he has worked out the doctrine of individualism in strict accord with the best teachings of contemporary science.

To many readers this novel will appeal as the latest expression of the literary art of the foremost living writer of fiction in English. They will make the inevitable comparison with "Feverel," "Harry Richmond," and "Diana," to see whether at sixty-seven the master's hand retains the old-time skill of the great artist. Whatever doubts they may have will vanish when they reach the chapter entitled "The Marine Duet." There the old fervor, the zest of living, the lyric quality of love, corruscate and sing and soar in language so strong, so musical, so inspiring, that the novelist is lost in the poet, and both in the emotion which they stimulate.

"THE MANXMAN"

A GREAT deal has been said in England against the three-volume novel as a work of art, as well as against its commercial qualities; and yet it has been responsible for a number of masterpieces in English fiction that surely would have failed of force and intellectual breadth if compressed into a single volume. It has no doubt produced great wastes of stupidity and dulness, but when you really come across a big fertile genius he needs three volumes in which to show his pace. You can't exhibit the qualities of an ocean "liner" on a frog-pond. There is a lot of satisfaction in reading a novel that is long enough to introduce you leisurely to a whole community, as well as to a pair of lovers. The intellectual "sprinting" that we call short stories and novelettes is good enough for mere cleverness. But it is boys' work after all, and is apt to stop growth of power and fancy.

When Hall Caine wrote "The Manxman," he had the advantage of a big canvas, and strength and force enough to fill it. The artistic effect of such a book is cumulative. The author can show his versatility without jarring your nerves by sudden changes of style and motive. The finest achievement in "The Manxman" is the creation of a lot of minor characters and incidents, which, though distinct in themselves, are inextricably woven into the great catastrophe. A small writer or a small volume would have deprived us of these. The detail of Manxland is as carefully worked into this story as Miss Wilkins's New England characteristics into her tales. It is applying the methods of modern realism to the creation of a romance.

The book to which "The Manxman" has been compared several times is "The Scarlet Letter"—because of a certain correspondence, with a contrast, in the motive. But it seems to me that there is far more reason to compare it artistically with "Adam Bede"—particularly as to the two women who sin—*Kate* and *Hetty*. There is a verity about these women—their rude beauty, their intensity, and their infatuations—that adds immensely to the attractions of a book which is, no doubt, often a bit repulsive in its remorseless pictures of human ignorance and weakness.

But the exhibition of the author's skill is in the development of the characters of *Philip* and *Pete*—a wonderful bit of psychology, which is pursued to its last analysis.

In spite of all this, a sensitive reader will feel that the novel has failed a little of the highest artistic effect. And he will trace the weak spot to the persistent effort to create scenes which are *theatrically* effective. The writer is always conscious of the stage-setting, the distribution of characters, and, as it were, the lime-light effects. Admirable as *Pete* is in conception and development, you are persistently aware of his wonderful advantages as a part for a romantic actor of big voice and handsome presence.

That sort of talent always commands a good audience, but it is not the best audience. Hugo and Dickens and Dumas pleased both the literary and dramatic audiences—but they are exceptions. You don't want to dramatize the novels of George Meredith or Thackeray. The foot-lights would kill the delicate fancy, the flights of imagination, the fascinating style that is the immortal part of them.

"TRILBY"

"TRILBY" is the beautiful story of three men who loved each other as brothers, and a woman who loved them all with that sort of comradeship that one expects from his dearest friend. That is why you have heard so many men talking about the story; for men, more than women, have a genius for comradeship. But you seldom find it in the modern novel, which is given over to the immature love of boys and girls, or to an analysis of the meannesses of men and women. But *Taffy*, the *Laird*, and *Little Billee* were bound together by that kind of friendship that seldom gets into books; you can't generalize about it or give recipes for it in platitudes. You only know that it can't be found among men who are without that depth and fidelity in their emotions which is called honor. It is not a matter of culture or æsthetics—for Kipling's "Soldiers Three" exhibit it in as admirable a manner as Du Maurier's "three guardsmen of the brush." Pleasure and good-fellowship may have had much to do with the beginnings of such comradeship, but, when it is once established, their office ends; for the test of comradeship is the hardships and the sorrows that are endured in its name. It is one of the permanent things of life that give it continuity. The beautiful thing about it all is that it carries with it none of those generally accepted obligations that are called duties. The whole relationship is so absolutely voluntary.

Now *Trilby* made her first appeal to these men, because she had the faculty of taking a man's views of comradeship. She saw what a genuine, unselfish thing it was; she grasped, what so many women of finer opportunities seldom understand — the meaning of honor among men. She did not ask them to pity, protect, or flatter or pet her (the appeal which most women make)—she simply said "Let me be your comrade on the same terms that you are each other's comrades. I ask no quarter because I am a woman." She had lost her honor among women, but she kept a man's standard of honor to the uttermost—" to think of other people before myself, and never to tell lies or be afraid."

But *Trilby* was a beautiful, magnetic woman, as well as a comrade, and so *Little Billee* and *Taffy* loved her with a great passion. One of them gave his life for it; the other, because he was stronger, grew to be a finer, nobler man by reason of it.

The four characters in this story have become to thousands of readers like real people. That is, perhaps, the highest tribute that one can pay to Du Maurier as a writer. His art has been so fine that he has made real for us his visions. The style of the narrative is so spontaneous, so unconventional that one feels that it is the veracious record of real experiences. Du Maurier is not afraid of his emotions—they bubble up and sparkle from a clear spring. They are not meant for analysis, but for enjoyment. That is why people are saying that he writes in the manner of the last generation. It is, one suspects, the sort of spontaneity that comes from hard work. The soul of the artist felt deeply, saw clearly, and then worked away with the instrument of language till his vision was made plain to others. *That* is not an easy thing to do; and the greater the artist, the harder the work. For he alone is fully conscious of the imperfections of language at its best to image the mind of man.

As for the hypnotic machinery of the story which evolves the two *Trilbys*, it is easy to overrate its originality and importance. As long ago as " The Blithedale Romance" of Hawthorne, and as recently as the " Dr. Jekyll and Mr. Hyde" of Stevenson, the dramatic possibilities of a dual personality were artistically treated in powerful romances. Du Maurier uses the device effectively, and in the very last chapter pushes it to the verge of melodrama, when *Trilby* dying is hypnotized by *Svengali's* picture.

The charm of the story is entirely apart from the machinery; it lies in the region of genuine emotion which springs from a zest for living. Notwithstanding its pathetic ending, the story is profoundly optimistic — for it breeds faith in human nature, respect for individuality, and a manly sympathy for error. It is such a lonely world to live in without these things—so lonely that when men lose faith in them all, they often voluntarily end their lives.

Stories like " Trilby " help to make it less lonely —for they give the emotions something to cling to—

> "A little warmth, a little light
> Of Love's bestowing—and so good-night!"

"TESS OF THE D'URBERVILLES"

TO tell a new story in an old manner, to be idyllic while unfolding a tragedy, to make the reader sympathize with a crime, to write a tale of the present day which is absolutely unconscious of railroads, telegraphs, and the worries of modern life—these are some of the anomalies in Thomas Hardy's novel, "Tess of the D'Urbervilles."

You are caught in the meshes of the tale before you realize it, and are carried to a romantic region. The sweet breath of the country is in your nostrils, and the winds from the Wessex valleys cool your brow. While you read there is no woman in the world but *Tess*, and to you, as to *Clare* in the light of early morning, she is no longer the milkmaid, but "a visionary essence of woman—a whole sex condensed into one typical form."

There is a Greek largeness and simplicity about *Tess* which is very appealing. The nervous subtleties of the modern woman are unknown to her. When she is happy it is an exaltation in which her strong body bears her up to a level plain of joy and keeps her there. About it there is nothing hysterical.

She has no imaginary sorrows; when they come, big, real, crushing, she puts her shoulders under them like a man, and struggles on—never stopping to whimper, or cry at fate. You realize that she is not indifferent, but is suffering keenly; that she thinks deeply as well as feels, and that she has an intellectual interest in the riddle of life.

You are never unconscious of the physical supremacy of *Tess*—the very womanly charm of her which accounts for so much that is both sad and happy in the story. "You are like an undulating billow warmed by the sun," said the infatuated *Clare* as he carried her, "and all this fluff of muslin about you is the froth." And that other picture of her, just waking from an afternoon sleep: "She was yawning, and he saw the red interior of her mouth as if it had been a snake's. She had stretched one arm so high above her coiled-up cable of hair that he could see its delicacy above the sunburn; her face was flushed with sleep, and her eyelids hung heavy over their pupils. It was a moment when a woman is more incarnate than at any other time."

Indeed, in the first four books of this novel it is hard to find a flaw. They are written in the wonderfully melodious English of which Hardy has long been an acknowledged master; the pastoral atmosphere saturates them; landscape after landscape springs into view and dissolves with the shifting of the breeze; and, above all, men and women live in this atmosphere and breathe the enchanted air. So far it is a beautiful romantic love-story, touching the deepest passions but permitting them to work out their own salvation.

Then, in what seems to be sheer perversity, the cloud of melodrama settles over the book. At one bound you are transported from the bracing air of the Wessex meadows to the stuffy atmosphere of a modern theatre. You can almost hear the shifting of the scenery, the whistle of the stage machinist, and see the changing color of the lights. The whole business of the tragedy is theatrical and unreal; the murder, the last happy night when *Tess* slept on the altar of the Druids, and the final scene of the black flag rising over the prison are cleverly devised stage pictures which would make the fortune of a different type of novel, but are utterly incongruous here.

The culmination of it all is a needless bit of cruelty. The reader closes the book with the impression that he has been defrauded of his sympathies, and he half-believes that the Home Secretary pardoned *Tess* at the last minute.

"THE PRISONER OF ZENDA"

THE wave of romance which has made the books of Stanley J. Weyman popular, has carried forward "The Prisoner of Zenda," by Anthony Hope (Hawkins). Most boys play at "being king," and this story carries on the play. Not only does the young Englishman play at being king, but he makes love to the real king's best girl. If there is anything more fascinating in romance than the king business, it is making love to a princess without any responsibility to marry her. Indeed, in the whole story the young Englishman has the best of the real king all the time. Of course he has to kill a few people now and then, but that is simply rare sport for a healthy Englishman.

Moreover, this story has lots of other stage properties of the old-fashioned sort. There is an unhealthy moat, and a drawbridge that creaks on its hinges, and a dungeon cell. In the human way, also, it is well supplied with gentlemanly assassins, treacherous confidential servants, and, better than all else, a beautiful but wicked woman, who loves the villain, but saves the life of his enemy.

What more can the children of the decade, who are

saturated with reality, ask for—unless it be a fairy godmother? There is a great deal to be said for fairy godmothers in a story. They make it easier for the novelist when he gets the plot tied into knots. The beautiful but wicked siren fills the part in a way in this tale, though she has her limitations. But a fairy godmother does not bother with the ordinary rules of the game. That is why we need to have her restored to full standing in the new school of old romance.

But, gentlemen of the new school, whatever you leave out of your stories, give us plenty of blood! Not ordinary blood spilt in brutal murders—we get enough of that in the newspapers—but fine blue blood shed in a gentlemanly way with plenty of "gadzooks" and "by my halidom" to accompany it. We have a preference for rapiers and broadswords as the weapons, because the reporters have made us suspect that a "Smith & Wesson 32 calibre" is a rather vulgar weapon.

We have nothing but praise for the way in which the hero of this story kills men. When it has to be done he makes clean work of it—even when he is compelled to run a knife into the man who is asleep in a boat.

We have only one fault to find with him—he ought to have run off with the beautiful princess. When he restored the real king to his kingdom he satisfied the moralities enough. The laws of romance demand that a genuine hero should be devilish enough to run away with a beautiful woman when he has the chance.

This is the only indication in the book that the modern Englishman has fallen away from the standard of the middle ages.

In the meantime, where is the American School of Romance? A contemporary cynic says that it is attending afternoon teas and kettledrums!

"SHIPS THAT PASS IN THE NIGHT"

THERE is something more satisfactory in the success of Miss Beatrice Harraden's stories, "Ships that Pass in the Night," and "In Varying Moods" than in tales of specious cleverness like "Dodo," for, at any rate, they are in dead earnest about a few things of some significance. Moreover, they are written with considerable respect for the English language as a vehicle for thought transference, and with a commendable knowledge of its best traditions. The style has an even, often a glittering edge on it, that cuts into the core of things, straight and clean. That is why people of small literary capability are pleased with the stories (they are so easily understood), and, at the same time people of some fastidiousness read them without shrugging their shoulders.

But what counts for the stories, more than all else, is the sense of reality which they convey. No amount of work or knowledge can give this; a writer either has the image-creating power, or he has not. If he has he will be read, even though he violates most of the laws of the English language, and all of the Ten Commandments. If the characters have reality, the reader will follow them, good or bad, to the end of the story. As *Wharton* says in "Marcella," you get the *thrill* from them and that is what most people are living for.

For example take the longest story in "In Varying Moods"—the first few pages domesticate the reader comfortably at the Green Dragon. He could find it without a map, and would recognize *Mrs. Benbow* at the door. That is a literary accomplishment of some importance at a time when many novels leave their characters in a haze at the very last chapter—the writers having expended most of their energy on the epigrams or social problems of the book, while the characters shifted for themselves.

But the thing which seems all wrong about Miss Harraden's stories is the attitude of the author and her people toward the often amusing spectacle which is called living. Almost without exception her stories end in death or heart-breaking renunciation. True, there is a certain stoicism about it all, which seems to say, "Of course, I am not making much fuss about this, but, ye gods, how I suffer!" If you are the right kind of a reader you are expected to aid in the silent suffering yourself. *That* is part of the thrill for which you paid.

But if you are a man or woman with the blood of health in your heart, you will say, after a little spasm of silent suffering, "How much better I should have felt if I had played two sets of tennis or taken a ten-mile ride! Some day, perhaps, I'll have to meet the real thing, and this simulation of it won't make me any braver." Or, maybe, "I endured tenfold these sorrows once myself, and this book reopens the old wound. Why did I read it?"

Of course if you are one of the melancholy contingent who make a profession out of sorrow (your own and other people's), we have nothing to say. "Ships that Pass in the Night" is just what you want; you'll get your own particular kind of thrill out of it, and plenty out of it.

But after you've read it, walk out on the hills at sunset, and let the breeze from off the wheat-fields play around your face, and take a deep breath when it has the perfume of clover in it; then watch the color glowing in the sky, and thank great nature that you are alive, and part of it all.

"KATHARINE LAUDERDALE"

THE easiest thing to say about an author who writes a great deal is that his latest book is not the equal of certain of his previous works; the particular one which a reader or critic selects for this comparison is always the book which happens to have left the most vivid impression on his mind. Now a vivid impression depends on so many things—on health for instance, on the pleasant surroundings, on the hour of the day, or the weather. That is why such comparisons are usually worthless. What does your opinion that " Mr. Isaacs " is a far better novel than " Katharine Lauderdale " amount to, when your friends know that in the ten years between the two you have not only grown older, but have lost your dearly beloved wife, or failed in your political ambition, or developed a persistent gout in your left foot?

Neither is it of any more significance for the writer to say that for him " Katharine " is a far better novel than " Mr. Isaacs " or any other novel Mr. Crawford ever wrote — except perhaps " Saracinesca " and " The Tale of a Lonely Parish "—just because the sun is shining when he writes after a week of snow and rain, and the birds are chirping in the square, and a bit of blue sky shows tremulously over the cornice across the street. The only safe thing, it seems, in judging of books, is to know why you like or dislike them, and leave comparisons alone.

You like "Katharine Lauderdale" no doubt because it is so thoroughly a modern story—and yet conscious of a dignified past, which is an inseparable part of the development of any society, even New York society. The valuable thing in Mr. Crawford's writing a New York story is that he has been in that city enough at long intervals really to see things at first hand, and yet he has been away so much in other great cities that he does not put things in that exaggerated perspective that in novels is called "provincialism." For a man may spend his whole life in a great city, and see the best that it affords, and yet be provincial in his judgments. No doubt there are many things in "Katharine" which real New Yorkers consider unessential or not in accord with the reality. There are also, no doubt, omissions of many things which New York considers the very essence of itself. But to many readers the very detachment of Mr. Crawford's view will be its chief charm.

"Katharine" is, moreover, charming for its dialogue, which is bright without being affected, crisp without being cynical. The people in the book preserve a reasonable dignity in their conversations with each other, and yet it is not "stage dignity," which so many novelists consider the real thing.

The achievement of the book, however, which will best stand all moods and weathers, is the admirable creation and characterization of the whole *Lauderdale* family—their evolution and present social dependencies. It is the first time in American fiction that any such breadth of view has shown itself in the study of our social framework. It suggests the opportunity for many other novels as good as this one. Mr. Crawford has shown very clearly that there is better material for stories of American life than the love agonies of detached young men and women, or the elaborately bad English of uninteresting people, which we call "dialect."

The story of "Katharine" is continued in "The Ralstons," a very long novel which succeeds in holding your attention in spite of an unusual number of digressions that seem to delay the plot.

It is not an agreeable story—the bickerings of the Lauderdale family being frequent and exceedingly irritating. But it is something of a task to show the strange results of an inherited family temper working in different personalities. There is a great deal of truth in this presentation of a strong family trait—one of the kind which makes the members of the family charming people to outsiders, but very annoying to each other. They have a keen appreciation of each other's virtues, but when brought together their eccentricities clash. They know it is foolish, but for their lives they cannot change it.

One of the best characters that the author has ever drawn is the old millionaire, *Robert Lauderdale*—a portrait of great strength, and unusual pathos of a virile kind. The chapters describing his illness and death are the best in the book—full of dignity and dramatic force.

THE "JUNGLE BOOK"

THE best book to write about is one that the critic has read with real enthusiasm; for then some of his enthusiasm, no matter how ill-natured he is, will creep into what he writes, and some one will read a stimulating book by reason of it. To that extent a critic may be, occasionally, a public benefactor. And that is why "The Jungle Book," by Rudyard Kipling, demands recognition. Kipling is so easily king among his fellows in a certain kind of narrative fiction, and has been so much praised that it is difficult to say anything new about him. But he has the astounding habit of always doing some entirely new thing in a strikingly original way. Therefore, even commonplace readers are moved to say new things about him.

Surely there is no prototype for "The Jungle Book" in either juvenile or grown-up literature. The nearest thing to it in English is "Uncle Remus," and the similarity goes no farther than the extraordinary way in which both Harris and Kipling get into the personality of animals and make them real and individual for the reader.

The book was in the main written for children, and one can imagine that a bright child would be fascinated with parts of it, even though the strange and uncouth words might be gibberish to him. For a child and a negro have an insatiable appetite for words with a big or curious sound. The prime condition is that they must suggest something to his imagination. There must be something wrong with a boy who would not sit up late to hear " Rikki-Tikki-Tavi " read to him; for the daring little mongoose who is the hero of the tale, possesses most of the virtues that a boy worships—fidelity to his chum, cunning in schemes to outwit his enemy, and bloodthirstiness in the presence of the foe.

But one fancies that grown-up boys, from twenty-five to sixty, will get most fun out of " The Jungle Book." And if they happen to know a little about the art of writing, their pleasure will be increased. For the book has some writing in it to make artists in the business jealous; for example, the night ride of little *Tomai* on the big elephant to the great elephant dance in the jungle. It is hard to find in Kipling a more weird or effective piece of description—the very soul of the jungle seems to be caught in it, and, for the time, you are part of an unknown world.

Of equal imaginative force is the story of " The White Seal "—perhaps the best story in the volume. It is a complete refutation of the charge that when Kipling leaves India he is out of his element, and his work falls off. This tale moves about in the depths of the sea, from the Arctic regions to the equator—and the reader is impressed with the same sense of reality that held him in the Indian jungle.

The book contains several incidental poems that perhaps meant something to little *Mowgli*, the wolf-child, but will puzzle the intellect of any one not educated by the Seeonee Pack. But even when they are obscure, you have a clear sense of the fact that nobody other than Kipling could have written them. Whatever he does he is always Kipling—and in dead earnest about his work.

"PEMBROKE"

IT is very easy to speak in unreserved praise of the technical ability in Miss Wilkins's novel "Pembroke." She never hesitates in conveying the impression of a scene or a situation as it is present to her mental vision; there it is, all set down on the page in direct, simple sentences that follow each other with the precision of soldiers on parade. Her style goes clipping and clicking its way through the pages like a well-geared and sharpened reaper through a field of wheat. Nothing is left for the reader's imagination, not even the gleanings. He simply sits on the fence and sees this efficient literary machine cut a broad swath through reality, bind it in orderly sheaves, and set them in a row. He may not like the grain, but there is nothing but admiration in his soul for the machine that is doing the work.

As for "Pembroke" itself—the obvious thing is to compare it with "Cranford." It conveys a similar sense of the reality of an insignificant village—and the unreality, and, moreover, unimportance of the rest of the world. While you are reading "Pembroke," there is no other standard of civilization or morality in your mind than Pembroke's. A writer of fiction can go no farther than that in the line of verity.

Moreover, with all its simplicity of life and character, the novel contains three or four scenes of real dramatic intensity—situations evolved as naturally as in life, and full of pathos and tragedy. With admirable restraint in language, these scenes are set down without a touch of the melodramatic. Pre-eminent among them are the flight of *Rebecca*, the journey of *Sylvia* to the poor-house, and the death of *Ephraim*. There is a severity, a sternness, an inevitableness in all these chronicles that suggest the Hebraic prototypes on which the old New England character was modelled.

There are two or three touches of moral allegory in the novel (like the veil over the face of *Sylvia*, and the imaginary crook in the back of *Barney*) that remind one of the methods of the great romancer who wrote "The Minister's Black Veil." This is a line of comparison which the most skilful of modern writers might hesitate to indicate.

The reader, not a New Englander, will close the book with admiration for the writer's skill, but with considerable satisfaction that his youth was not spent in a New England village. It is doubtful whether more disagreeable people were ever gathered in a single novel (outside of "Wuthering Heights") than in "Pembroke." The first hundred pages of the book are a record of family bickering and quarrels in three households—in which brothers and sisters, and mothers and fathers are arrayed against each other in the name of the Lord. We have been told in New England-made histories that it is from homes like these that the strong men, the "makers of the Republic," in politics, literature, and art, have sprung.

One can imagine *Colonel Carter* saying, after reading "Pembroke," "By gad, sah, we may not be makahs of the Republic, sah, but we know how to live respectably, affectionately, and honorably with our own people!"

"DAVID BALFOUR"

IT is a very trying test of the growth and performance of a writer when he publishes the sequel to a great success after a long interval. Robert Louis Stevenson set up such a standard for judgment when he published the sequel to "Kidnapped"—the memoirs and adventures of "David Balfour." The critical reader may hold himself in this attitude of judgment for the first hundred pages of "David Balfour." For that space he will admire chiefly the admirable technic of the novel. He will marvel most of all, perhaps, at the intellectual dexterity with which Stevenson put himself, body and soul, into the Scotland of 1751, and then proceeded, with the ease of an eighteenth-century Scotchman, to write four or five Scotch dialects in the same chapter—Highland and Lowland, chief and peasant, Fife and Lothian—each differing from the other by some gradations of pronunciation, some words and phrases peculiar to the class or clan. The finest manifestation of this accomplishment is the ease and perfect naturalness with which *Balfour*, for example, changes his mode of speech to suit the character he is addressing—and, little by little, all the while reveals the steps of his own development, from an awkward village boy to a man of the world, with some social graces. Whether or not this linguistic jugglery was the fruit of a scholar's knowledge of the period, or a feat of the imagination, can only concern one or two learned Scots at the most. For the critical reader it is enough to feel that Stevenson did a very difficult thing, with an air of truth and reality which needed no further justification.

After the first hundred pages all these questions of technic and literary skill are swept out of sight by the glamour of the romance. From there to the end it is *Catriona* and *David*, *Alan Breck* and *James More* who are the real and pertinent things to you. *Catriona* is henceforth one of the charming and lovable women you are glad to have known. She refutes for all time the charge that the author could not create a womanly woman. Her charm is the directness and fidelity of her affection; but the spice is her nimble Scotch temper, which flames up like burning heather in a drought, and then glows long with the warmth of it, like smouldering peat. "There's just the two sets of weemenfolk," says *Alan Breck*, "them that would sell theer coats for ye, and them that never look the road ye're on. That's a' that there is to women." And that's a big part of *Catriona*, but not all, *Alan* my braw lad; there is an amazing amount of Scotch pride in her which makes her own personal independence (what men call honor) of more account to her than the love of *David*. She would not have his love unless it came to her without a shade of false motive.

Alan comes nearer all the truth in summing up the character of *David Balfour*—"He's no very bonnie, my dear, but *he's leal to them he loves.*"

The tendency of recent writing has been to put loyalty to an abstract principle ahead of personal loyalty. We have been making heroes of men who renounce family and friends for the sake of a creed. This is, no doubt, a great force for progress, but one must confess that there never was a finer cloak for hypocrisy, treachery, and selfishness than this same "loyalty to a principle." Oh, the friends and homes that have been sacrificed to feed the vanity of it! It's a fine thing to put on a tombstone that a man was loyal to his principles; but in his heart of hearts a decent man would rather have it written of himself, living or dead—"He's leal to them he loves."

THE LITERARY PARTITION OF SCOTLAND

THE LITERARY PARTITION OF SCOTLAND

IN the present partition of Scotland for literary purposes among fiction writers, the following amicable allotment of territory seems to have been agreed upon : Forfarshire to Barrie, Inverness and Ross to William Black, Fife to Annie Swan and the author of " Barncraig," Perthshire to Ian Maclaren, and old Galloway to S. R. Crockett. So long as each keeps to his own territory these brethren dwell together in unity and unstintedly praise each other's books. Instead of the old feuds of the clans, these modern chieftains seem to have formed a Literary Trust for Scotland which runs things to suit itself and absorbs the bulk of the profits in the business of making marketable tales. As they have a monopoly of the brains adapted for that kind of work, there is no particular reason why they should not have the emoluments.

But some of these days a venturesome young Scot, who has been fighting his way through Edinburgh University on sixpence a day, will put on his bonnet and kilt, gird on his dagger and slip a skene-dhu into his stocking. Then he will sally forth into the literary territory of one of the present chieftains, and there will be as pretty a fight in the literary way as has been seen since the old days of Christopher North.

In the meantime, Americans will buy unlimited quantities of the books of chieftains and usurpers, and, with their usual indifference, will become more familiar with the traditions, history, and dialects of a country three thousand miles away than with their own States. And they are little to blame for it, because many of our own writers, as soon as they become tolerably adept in the business, are apt to go abroad and spend the rest of their days "discovering" European types and writing about them. The American reader, with his usual acuteness, prefers the real foreign novel to an imitation of it by one of his countrymen; and he is about right in his preference.

J. M. BARRIE

J. M. BARRIE is one of the group of Scots who are writing so much of the good poetry, essays, and fiction which come from over the sea. Lang, MacDonald, Black, Buchanan are his older fellow-countrymen, each with a style of his own—for whatever else a Scot may be in his writings, he is usually a stylist. He is rather a man of feeling, of enthusiasm, than of remarkable intellectual culture—and it is feeling that gives individuality to style.

To get at what is best in Barrie's earlier work one must read "A Window in Thrums" and "Auld Licht Idylls"—a series of sketches, lightly caught together by the reappearance of the same characters from time to time, and all of them centred in the Scotch village of Thrums—"a handful of houses jumbled together in a cup," where twenty years ago nearly every man was a weaver, working out his life over a handloom. They were a solemn people to whom the most serious thing in life was the Kirk, and the only social division, the impassable moral barriers that divided Auld Lichts from Free Kirks and U. Ps.

The quality which Mr. Barrie puts into his sketches of this quaint old village life is entire absorption in it. For him and for his reader there is no other place, no other standard of judgment than Thrums. It is his aloofness from any larger interests that makes Thrums so real. You are living with him in the house at the top of the brae and see the world through *Jess's* window. It is a gray world, narrow and sad and filled with poverty. But there is a certain moral elevation about the people, a brave attitude toward the worst that life can bring, which gives distinction to them. Poverty or occupation has nothing to do with the essential refinement of a family like *Jess* and *Hendry* and *Leeby*. Their heart-breaking affection for each other, which conceals itself behind a stolid manner, their consideration in little things, their determination to endure cheerfully—these are the qualities which would make any station in life dignified.

It would be hard to choose between the pathos and humor of these books—for each is so simple, direct, and natural. They chase each other from page to page, treading on each other's heels. You are never conscious that the author is playing with your feelings —for all that happens is so necessary.

This does not imply that the sketches are uniformly successful; for they may be colorless like "Davit Lunan's Political Reminiscences," or, perhaps, too farcical, like the "Auld Lichts in Arms."

But at their worst, the charm of the homely style,

with its Gaelic idioms giving it both strength and melody, will carry the reader through them with delight.

Barrie's "My Lady Nicotine" is a book that suggests but is very unlike "The Reveries of a Bachelor." The former is urban; the latter is provincial. A brier pipe filled with Arcadia Mixture starts the reveries in the one; a hearth fire, in the other.

The five bachelors in "My Lady Nicotine" seem to be utterly dissimilar in tastes and feelings—and have only one bond of union, their common love for the famous Arcadia Mixture. The solemnity with which they treat their pipes; their assured superiority to everybody outside of the circle which knows and appreciates that mysterious brand of tobacco; the sentimental selfishness of their bachelor existence, and the delicate humor with which the quiet episodes are narrated—these are some of the charming qualities of the book.

But the crowning humor of it is that the story is told by one of their number, who boldly announces in the first chapter that he has married, and that his wife has won him from his pipe and his comrades. He cheaply moralizes on their enslavement, and then in reveries calls up the happy days when he smoked with them.

The closing chapter is a most subtle piece of writing. The narrator praises his constancy to his promise never to smoke again, and adds: "I have not even any craving for the Arcadia now, though it is a tobacco that should only be smoked by our greatest men." Then he confesses that when his wife is asleep and all the house is still, he sits with his empty brier in his mouth, and listens to the taps of a pipe in the hands of a smoker (whom he has never seen) on the other side of the wall. "When the man through the wall lights up I put my cold pipe in my mouth and we have a quiet hour together."

Barrie's most ambitious work is, of course, his novel, "The Little Minister." The style is flexible, penetrating, rough but melodious—the product of an early saturation with Burns, the Bible, and Rous's version of the Psalms. There are in it also touches of contemporary literary godfathers, for you may catch a trace of Stevenson with his "love of lovely words" in Barrie's choice of names like Windyghoul and Glen Quharity; and from no other man than George Meredith could he have learned so well the art of mingling an intense emotional crisis with what is unusual and uncanny in nature—like the great rain-storm through which the culmination of this story moves. You are made to see the Windyghoul and the Glen through the emotions of the actors in the drama, and not as an artist sees a landscape with an eye for color and detail and composition.

In the way of character also you catch a hint of Meredith's methods; you inevitably think of *Kiomi*, the gypsy girl, in "Harry Richmond," when *The Egyptian* of this story appears. But these things are the faintest echoes—for of all men Barrie is original.

His *Tammas Whamond* is a creation who might be admitted to illustrious companionship with the great *Mulvaney*—and while *Mulvaney* would brag of the time when he was "a sergeant and a divil of a man," *Whamond* would wrap himself up in the "mantle of chief elder o' the Kirk."

It is more in the minor characters than the principals that the quality of the story is shown. You are made to know these people, who come and go without evident reason, as you would know them if you lived in the village of Thrums and saw them every Sabbath in the Auld Licht Kirk. You begin to judge the Little Minister by their standard, and develop a small prejudice against the U. Ps. and the Free Kirk.

What you will oftenest recall with pleasure is the delicious humor of certain episodes — like *Waster Lunny* frantically searching for the book of Ezra; or piper *Campbell's* mighty wrath when he was ordered by the Earl to play the "Bonny House o' Airlie"— the tune which the Ogilvys used to hurl at the clan Campbell; or *The Egyptian's* first meeting with the *Little Minister*, and how she outwitted him.

Indeed the book must be judged rather as a series of character sketches (like "A Window in Thrums" and the "Auld Licht Idylls") than as a full-fledged novel. It is a charming piece of work, interesting from first to last, but lacking in unity. And there is the gentle spirit of *Margaret* which pervades the book—"one whose nature was not complex, but most simple, as if God had told her only to be good."

OF all the morbid novels that are now being written and read there is not a single one coming from this group of clever Scotchmen. Therefore you may read "The Raiders," by S. R. Crockett, with confidence that you will not think worse of your race when you have finished it. It is like a strong, fresh breeze from the heathery hills, with the bracing touch of salt water clinging to it. There is a deal of blood and fighting in it—and you can almost take it as an axiom that the more pious the origin of a Scotch writer the more gore will you find in his novels. It is probable that the long chapters from the Old Testament committed to memory in boyhood give their minds a turn toward fighting and conflict. And then, too, there is atavism to account for it—the reappearance in the third or fourth generation of the old ways, when the clans chased each other like hounds and only the strong men survived. It was very brutal no doubt, but, physiologically speaking, it was a good way to rid a whole race of weaklings.

A very good argument could be made by any man (not a Scotchman) to prove that there is nothing elevating in literature that devotes itself to the brutal struggles of strong men with each other; that a prize-fight is a prize-fight, whether it is described by Robert Louis Stevenson or the New York *World*. There is no doubt a touch of barbarism in it, but it stirs your blood in the right way. After you have read the fight on the Brig of Dee in "The Raiders," you'll have no stomach for "The Yellow Aster" or "Dodo." Between barbarism and a jaundiced soul, the sane man will choose barbarism every time.

All of which does not admit, for an instant, that "The Raiders" is barbaric. It is really elevated in sentiment and motive. The love of the *Laird of Rathan* and *May Mischief* is poetic, and strong as well. The steadfastness of *Silver Sand* is real heroism. And so throughout the book, the sentiments and motives are vigorous and full of health. It is easy to trace the literary ancestry of the book. The author himself has frankly paid homage to Stevenson. A clever man recently said that "The Raiders" was the offspring of *Alan Breck* and *Lorna Doone*, which surely indicates its salient qualities. At the same time it sets the standard of judgment very high, and the story falls short in some particulars. For one thing, the tale often flounders around in pages of wordy descriptions which lead to nothing.

The archaisms have something to do with this effect. Not only is it Scotch, and Galloway Scotch at that, but it is the language of the early part of the eighteenth century. The author has evidently spared no pains to be correct in his dialect. He must be credited with a considerable intellectual accomplishment, but the reader who is not a philologist will long for less of the archaic and more good English.

But with it all one's fancy is refreshed by reading the story, and there is a touch of color left in one's memory that was never there before.

Another of Mr. Crockett's novels, "Mad Sir Uchtred of the Hills," keeps close to the Galloway hills and the days of the Covenanters.

It isn't a pleasant tale, and no amount of archaic Scotch, with a sprinkling of psalm-singing and long prayers, can seriously interest a reader in a mad, unkempt, naked, and dirty old chief who is playing Nebuchadnezzar on the hills, while his brother makes love to his wife at home.

The one touch of beauty in the story is the faithful *Philippa* with her children—all of them shadowy sketches, leaving the tale without that leaven of idyllic love which softened the harshness of "The Raiders."

The reaction from "prettiness" in writing is a good thing; but this is not a barbarous age, and a great deal can be said for the doctrine of the late Walter Pater as to the supremacy of beauty in life and art. Surely it ought to count for a good deal in the literary art!

It is probable that some of the success of Mr. Crockett is due to the fact that his books and favorite characters do not offend against the accepted standards of morality as handed down from generation to generation of decent people. Moreover, they actually approve of these standards heartily, and bring to severe punishment those who go against them. Such an attitude in a fiction-writer would not have attracted attention a few years ago—because it was taken for granted that he approved of such things before he went into the business.

But some daring Englishman (probably George Moore, first of all), took the other tack, achieved notoriety, and, for three or four years since, the man or woman who wrote a book to upset some accepted standard was pretty sure of success.

In a literary period pretty generally occupied with kicking over the traces, a good, steady-going Scotch dominie, with considerable of the preacher's knack at parables, has achieved a success which seems out of proportion to his literary output. He has written, as we have said, one book of force and originality—"The Raiders"—and three or four other studies of Galloway character that are put into attractive English interlarded with barbaric Scotch dialect. But there is nothing in all this to justify the opinion that the sacred fire that went out in Samoa is rekindled upon his hearth.

Indeed, his recent story, "The Play Actress," is a ludicrous illustration of what may result from a provincial minister's attempting to prove that he is a literary man of broad equipment, "in touch with the world," by writing a story in which glimpses are given of the wickedness of London.

IAN MACLAREN

A NEW Scotch writer has come out of Perthshire to enter the quaint town of Drumtochty into competition with Thrums as a centre of literary interest. In "Beside the Bonnie Brier Bush" Ian Maclaren has done some very good writing of the simple, direct sort that comes natural to Scotchmen. The old, quaint types are also in its pages—men and women with hard, strong faces, under which are playing deep feeling and imagination. They are good people to know in either books or real life, though they are often rather trying (in both places), by reason of their tremendous respect for their own personality and persistent undervaluing of the personality of alien people. One may sincerely praise Mr. Maclaren for his very genuine grasp of the things that make character in simple folks, and for the strong, expressive English in which he sets down his impressions. He shows a true sense of the literary value of common things in a lack of exaggeration and in utter obliviousness to any other standard of life or manners than that of Drumtochty. One is inclined to think that what he imagines to be real pathos is sometimes rather forced, and his heroism, a kind of inevitable obstinacy. But the sketch of the village doctor is of great force and naturalness. It is one of the best stories of Scotch humble life of recent years.

VII

FRIENDS IN ARCADY

CHARLES DANA GIBSON

FOR a good many years the writer has furnished articles to be set in type and used as frames around the drawings of C. D. Gibson. When he has constructed a paragraph that filled his heart with joy and vanity, it has been his luck to open next week's *Life* and find that a Gibson Girl had put her dainty foot right through the middle of it. There has been no subject in contemporary literature upon which the present writer has attempted to shed light that the Gibson Girl has not intruded some part of her anatomy or finery into it. She has done it very gracefully and with a ravishing smile; but even that won't smooth out the creases in a writer's vanity when he finds his choicest sentences cut in two by a picture.

At last a day of reckoning and revenge has arrived. Mine enemy has published a book—"Drawings by Charles Dana Gibson."

The trouble with revenge for which one has waited a long time is that it isn't sweet. The edge is off the grievance, and one has endured it so long that it takes the guise of a blessing. So it happens that I have come to look upon the Gibson Girl as my friend. I am positive that she has broken up more stupid paragraphs than bright ones—for all of which I am duly thankful.

Indeed, the Gibson Girl, as she appears in this volume, is a charmer to melt the heart of any crusty bachelor. Even my friend the cynical Adrian says that she is "no clothes' horse." She is dressed *à la mode* to be sure, but she has a pair of shoulders under her coat that can drive an oar through the water or keep a hunter down to his work. And her neck rises out of her gown as though it were attached to something substantial. Then she looks square at you with intelligent eyes that hide a touch of mischief lurking in their corners. She is healthy and brave and independent and well-bred ; she can dance as well as she can run a Boys' Club, and she knows as much about golf as French and German. She goes to church on Sundays, recites the Ten Commandments, and reads *Life* every Tuesday. That is the Girl as I know her. She is probably different to you. At any rate you will find her somewhere in this volume. You can't miss it ; if you own this book you'll have a picture of your ideal girl.

For Gibson has a way of adopting all nice girls into his family. You don't realize what a large family he has until you get them all together in this book. There is a proud and haughty beauty among them that only a millionaire, with a superb education in addition to his bank account, would dare propose to. And then there is a pleasant-faced, black-eyed fascinator, who would not mind living in a cheap house in the suburbs if she really loved a man. She would make the man believe that he owned a magnificent villa, and was the happiest fellow in New Jersey.

Mr. Gibson has a great responsibility on his shoulders, and if he once fully realizes it, it will keep him awake nights. I wonder if he knows that there are thousands of American girls, from Oshkosh to Key West, who are trying to live up to the standard of his girls. You can always tell when a girl is taking the Gibson Cure by the way she fixes her hair. I've watched them go through the whole scale from Psyche knots, to Pompadour, to Bath Buns, to side waves with a bewitching part in the middle.

Then, too, he has set a most adorable fashion in widows. I know sane, intelligent bachelors who prefer the Gibson Widow to the Girl. The trouble with the Widow is that she is so transitory. You are dead certain that she is just waiting to be asked, and that you are the man to ask her.

Now a real Art Critic would not tell you about the girls and the widows in Gibson's book, but would give you a lot of information about the wonderful technic, the simplicity of line, the grace of composition, the freedom, the directness, etc. I've heard men say who know (and real critics all know), that Gibson has all of those things, and a good many more. And I believe he has; but he does not make much fuss about them. He goes right along making better and better pictures, working with energy and intelligence—and the other fellows do the talking.

A. B. FROST

I ONCE heard the editor of a humorous paper say that A. B. Frost was the best caricaturist in America, and that he often picked up his series of sketches called "The Humane Man and the Bull Calf" and looked them over in order to have a good laugh. Now there must be something in the work of a man who can make the editor of a humorous paper laugh outside of business hours. Hopkinson Smith, in trying to explain psychologically why we laugh at Mr. Frost's caricatures, says that "no man laughs effectively with pen or brush who does not laugh with his own soul first"—thus implying that, among his other admirable possessions, Frost owns a laughing soul. That seems like a good explanation, but, as I don't know anything about Mr. Frost's soul, I asked him about it, and he replied that "Bunner's article about me in *Harper's Magazine*, for October, 1892, contains all the facts." I looked it up and found that Mr. Bunner believed that "honesty" was the principal characteristic of Frost's art—that it is honest clear through, including its "American atmosphere." I always suspected that Mr. Frost was honest, and I'm glad to find it confirmed by one of his friends—but somehow that does not help to explain why we laugh at his pictures. I've known some very good men who laughed at pictures made by rogues.

It's a very good start, though, toward our understanding of Mr. Frost to know that he is "honest" and has a "laughing soul," but I suspected that his models had something to do with the real funniness of his pictures, and I asked him about it.

"I use *one* model for all my men," he replied. "I rarely have more than one model for old and young, black or white. If I could get a model for every figure I draw I would do so, but it is out of the question with such rapid work as illustration. I might mention that there is a singular peculiarity about the women; all the handsome ones are stupid and can't put an idea into a pose, and all the bright ones who can and will pose and help your work are decidedly plain both as to face and figure. I have never been able to get much satisfaction out of the surrounding rural population as models. I have tried the local picturesque old men, with the result of having them go to sleep when I gave them a comfortable pose, and having them wriggle all the time when I didn't. The local small boy is better, but he is always sent in his Sunday clothes, in which he is far from picturesque."

As a great deal of Mr. Frost's work is done for the magazines about six months before the date of publication, this question of models is still further complicated with the necessity of getting the honest American atmospheric effect that Mr. Bunner praises. One August, when the thermometer stood about 90°, even on the hills of Madison, N. J., where Mr. Frost lives, he had a fine run of work for the Christmas magazines that demanded night snow-scenes for a steady background. So for several weeks the artist used to retire to his studio, darken the windows, and study night effects in a stifling atmosphere. It is no wonder that the rural population of Morris County are a trifle restless and unsatisfactory as models.

Every one knows how realistic are the animals in Frost's pictures, with infinite variety in pose and expression—revealing many degrees of emotion, as those will remember who have seen the series known as "Violet's Experience." He has confessed the secret of this success: "I have a very fat white bull-dog who has learned to pose. My man holds him for a while till he is settled down, and then he seems to know what I want and will keep his position for a long time, looking beseechingly at me every now and then. When I am through and give him the word he will bounce about and bark delightedly, and then go out as soon as possible. One pose is enough for him."

Mr. Frost does not say that the white bull-dog poses for the whole animal kingdom, just as the one man poses for all humanity, but it is a fair inference, and certainly helps to confirm the "laughing-soul" theory of Mr. Smith.

Another thing which makes Mr. Frost's soul laugh is when people solemnly ask him, "Do you *read* the story you are illustrating?" "I wonder whether they think I know it by intuition," he said to a friend, "or whether I sit up nights with the author and have him tell me."

As Mr. Frost is very fond of the country and of animals, it is natural that he should have taken recently to doing sporting pictures, and has a number of subjects which he is working up. He is personally fond of shooting, but gets little time to go long distances from home where game abounds. On those rare occasions when he combines sketching with his shooting trips he meets with amusing, though often annoying experiences, many of which have found their way into his humorous sketches. "They always speak of a landscape as 'a scenery,' and tell you where there are much better 'sceneries,'" he says. One old boy came every day to watch him as he was painting a study of some cherry-trees, and professed a great love for pictures and praised Frost's work highly. After a long harangue about art and his fondness for it, the old man said one day: "Do you know, if had a hundred thousand dollars I believe I'd be durn fool enough to *buy* some of them things."

"On another occasion," says Mr. Frost, "I was trying to paint a sunset, and, having made a failure of my sketch, I scraped it off the canvas and told a farmer who had been watching me for some time that

I had not worked quick enough to get the effect. After some consideration he replied, 'Wall, why don't two or three of yez go at it at onct?'"

One reason why Mr. Frost's pictures are always humanly interesting and fresh in subject and idea is that not only does he work steadily and very hard, but he manages to get his fun along with his work. That means that his art and his life are thoroughly united, and he never will have regrets that in following art he perhaps missed life, or in living happily he perhaps missed art. Work has been his normal condition from the day when, fifteen years old, he went into the employ of an engraver in Philadelphia and began to learn the art by running errands. In less than a year he took up lithography, and worked at it for five or six years. Mr. Frost was fortunate in having for a friend William J. Clarke, a brother of the humorist who wrote under the name "Max Adeler," and he insisted that Frost should illustrate his brother's book, "Out of the Hurly-Burly," which he did to the delight of the author and the public. Mr. Bunner says they are very bad wood-cuts, "that look as if they were carved with a penknife" (which was not Frost's fault), but I remember laughing over them many an evening when I was a boy—and all the other boys did likewise. That was the beginning of Frost's career as an illustrator, which soon brought him to New York to work on the *Graphic;* and in 1876 he joined Abbey, Reinhart, and Alexander at Harper's. He had taken drawing lessons at the Philadelphia Academy of Fine Arts in the evenings, but in 1877 decided to get a more thorough training by going to England. In a year he returned to the United States, and settled down to steady work near Philadelphia, where he was married in 1883.

Mr. Frost makes his home on the top of a hill near Madison, where the "sceneries" are a good crop, raised on a farm of about one hundred and forty acres, with a house in the middle of it that has big pillars along the front.

Mr. Frank R. Stockton is a neighbor of Mr. Frost's. He also is a farmer when he is not trying to solve the riddle of "The Lady or the Tiger?" If you ask Mr. Stockton about Frost he'll tell you that Frost is one of the best fellows and best artists in the world—but no farmer. "Why, he tried to sell me what he called a first-class horse last summer, and you could hear his joints rattle when he walked. Besides he is no judge of cows."

If you ask Frost about Stockton he'll tell you that he is the best of neighbors and writes boss stories—"but he's no farmer. He offered to sell me one of his first-class cows, and I had to ask him whether a set of false teeth went with the cow, before he saw that I would not buy her. Besides, Stockton is no judge of horses."

And this is the end of the chapter, and nothing has been said about the large amount of admirable work on which Mr. Frost's great reputation as an illustrator is built. But everybody knows about that, for everybody has seen his pictures in Stockton's "Rudder Grange," Lewis Carroll's "Phantasmagoria," Octave Thanet's "Stories of a Western Town," Munkittrick's "Farming," Bunner's "Story of a New York House," and Frost's own books "Stuff and Nonsense" and "The Bull Calf and Other Tales." If you say nice things about his illustrations to him he will hear you patiently, and then quizzically reply: "Yes, but like every other illustrator under the sun, I want to be a painter."

F. MARION CRAWFORD

THERE is no need to localize this conversation with F. Marion Crawford, for he is equally at home in a dozen great cities of the world. The readers of his books do not need any particular background to explain the man; he is a thorough cosmopolite. But personally I have always thought of Mr. Crawford as working in a grotto under the cliffs of Sorrento, with the flashing waters of the bay shining through the arched opening, and the little waves playing on the white sand, almost at his feet. There I have often imagined him sitting before a little square and much-worn table of pine, with nothing on it but reams of paper and a bottle of ink, and on one corner, near his hand, a teapot, under which the pale blue flame is always burning. I have pictured him there, day after day, drinking unnumbered cups of tea, and summoning out of the dark recesses of the grotto the strange and romantic company who are his familiars — *Paul Patoff, Dr. Claudius, Saracinesca, Gouache, Mr. Isaacs, Ram Lal, Marzio, Zoroaster.* They spring from the darkness, talk with him awhile, disappear and reappear, forming dramatic groups and doing daring deeds. And, while they come and go, he is always writing, writing, imperturbably writing, even when talking with them. I do not know where I first got this idea, but I think I can trace it to a chapter in "To Leeward" and a chance newspaper paragraph. At any rate, I have been a firm believer in that grotto for many years, and I want to continue to believe in it. Since I have known Mr. Crawford personally, I have carefully avoided asking him about it, for I don't want to destroy the illusion, if it is one, and I don't believe it *is* an illusion. With each new novel of his that I have read, I have seen the grotto grow a little larger, the darkness become more populous. I used to think that on some sunny day I should be rowed across the bay of Sorrento (perhaps by one of the "Children of the King"), and should be landed from the little boat at the very mouth of the cave; and then I should introduce myself to Mr. Crawford, and be asked to have a cup of tea and a smoke. When we had talked awhile, I hoped he would summon his familiars from the darkness to smoke and talk with us. *That* is where and how this conversation should have taken place.

But there are some things that even a romantic novelist cannot do, though Thackeray said that "anything you like happens in Fable-land." So we were compelled to talk in a room, in the heart of New York, which had little in it except books, and a big chair, and a blaze of cannel-coal in the grate. If you fill the big chair with Mr. Crawford, smoking an

English bull-dog pipe in which is some of Barrie's "Arcadia Mixture," you will have all the background that is needed for this conversation.

"You know," he said, "that my father, Thomas Crawford, was a Scotch-Irishman, born in the West of Ireland, and brought to this country when very young. His father acquired a small business in New York which supported him comfortably, and he wished his son, my father, to take part in it; but the boy had a strong artistic bent, and of his own initiative went to a wood-carver to learn his trade. Later, wishing still greater freedom for his skill, he learned marble-carving, and, by a curious coincidence, he designed the handsome mantels in the house of Mr. Ward, his future father-in-law, at the corner of Bond Street and Broadway. This and other of his work was so remarkable that my grandfather and his friends determined that he should have the best opportunities to study sculpture, and he was sent to Rome, where he was a pupil of the great Thorwaldsen. While a young sculptor in Rome, gaining recognition every day, he met Miss Louisa Ward, who was travelling with Dr. Samuel G. Howe and his wife, Julia Ward Howe. They fell in love and were married, and made Rome their home. I am the youngest of their four children. When I was about two years old (in 1856) I was sent to this country, and lived with some kinsfolk on a farm near Bordentown, N. J. Among the earliest things that I remember is my great delight in watching the coming and going of the trains of cars as they shot across the farm near the old house. My father died in London, in 1857, when I was three years old, and soon after I was taken back to Italy, where all my youth was spent."

I asked Mr. Crawford to tell me about his education as a boy. It seemed to recall a host of pleasant recollections.

"Most of my boyhood was spent under the direction of a French governess. Not only did I learn that language from her, but all of my studies, geography, arithmetic, etc., were taught me in French, and I learned to write it with great readiness as a mere boy, because it was the language of my daily tasks. The consequence is that to this day I write French with the ease of English. There have been times when I knew that I had lost some of my facility in speaking French, through long absence from the country; but the acquirement of writing it is always with me, which shows the value of early impressions in that direction."

I remembered hearing St. Paul's School men speak of the days when Mr. Crawford was a student at Concord, N. H., and I asked him when he had been there.

"I was about twelve years old," he said, "when I was sent over to America again, and went to St. Paul's. There I found that the fact that I had been taught Latin by a natural, and not an artificial method, gave me a great advantage. My Latin tutor in Rome was a man whose ideas of learning that language were most original then, although they have since become more common in certain systems. I remember that my first lesson in Latin was to read one of the very short letters of Cicero, only two or three lines. We began by reading, and, as a consequence, I was interested from the very first lesson. You know that in Rome you are surrounded with Latin inscriptions on the public buildings and monuments, so that the whole language had a reality to me that it could hardly have to an American boy, especially one who has learned it by way of the rudiments of grammar."

We had a long talk about the various steps in his education, which seemed to be full of pleasant memories for Mr. Crawford. He recalled his student days with a clergyman in the English village of Hatfield Regis, and the gayer life at Trinity College, Cambridge, where he went in for boating, and, incidentally, for mathematics. "They thought I was a mathematician in those days," he said. Then followed student days at Karlsruhe and Heidelberg, from 1874 to 1876. "Of course," he said, "I learned my German in those days—learned to speak it readily; but I have never acquired the ability to write it as fluently as I do French."

"And then," he continued, "I studied at the University of Rome (1876–78), and I had a tutor who taught me Sanskrit, and interested me in Buddhism and other Oriental mysteries. There came a time when my people lost a great deal of money, and

I was in a quandary what to do. This tutor advised me to take an opportunity to go to India and learn Sanskrit, and then I could come back and easily get a good professorship. So, with the enthusiasm of youth, I borrowed one hundred pounds, and sailed for Bombay. But money seemed to be as hard to earn in Bombay as elsewhere. I tried in vain for all sorts of positions. I wrote occasionally articles for a Bombay newspaper, and made the acquaintance of the editor, but these were not enough to replenish my stock of money. One day I found myself reduced to my last two pounds, and I could not see where more was coming from; but I was young and strong, and I said that if the worst came, I could enlist in the British army, and have plenty of adventure, and food and clothes. I sat down and wrote a letter of application to the proper officer, sealed and stamped it, and held it in readiness to mail when I should find that there was nothing else to be done. The next day I received a letter from the editor of the *Bombay Gazette*, asking me to call. When I presented myself, he said that he had received a letter from the proprietor of the *Allahabad Indian Herald*, asking whether he could send him immediately a good man to take charge of that paper. He explained to me that it was a very difficult undertaking, as I should have to do all the editorial work myself; that Allahabad was a thousand miles away; and that, in certain seasons, the climate was disagreeable and dangerous. Nevertheless he asked me would I go? 'Would a duck swim?' I said, and started immediately. I found that the paper was a daily, issued every afternoon. I was my own news collector, managing editor, and editorial writer. I wrote a leading article and several editorial paragraphs every day, collected and wrote the local news, edited the correspondence from all over India—some of it written in the worst English that I have ever encountered. There were days when I worked sixteen hours at a stretch; there were days at the beginning of the rainy season when the combination of heat and moisture was enough to drive a man who had nothing to do to an extremity. How much worse it was, you can imagine, when one had to work sixteen hours in that atmosphere, and that, too, in daily journalism, an occupation in which I had had no experience whatever."

I said that it reminded me of a story of Kipling's.

"Yes," he replied, "'The Man who would be King'—that is it exactly. I always read Kipling with a flood of recollections of India, so true are his stories to the reality. Of course," he said, "I picked up a great deal about Buddhism and other oriental lore, and it was at Simla that I met the original of *Mr. Isaacs*—a real man whose name was Jacobs. Of him I shall tell you by and by. For eighteen months I edited the *Indian Herald*, and I think it was the hardest work that I have ever done. By and by, in 1880, I returned to Italy, and there I again found myself without means or work, so I took passage on an old steamer for America, early in 1881.

I was the only cabin passenger on board. The boat was a regular tramp; we struck terrible storms, the machinery broke down, and under sail we slowly made our way westward. I had always been fond of the sea, and, as the ship was short-handed, I took my watch, turn and turn about, with the captain and the mates. After six weeks we got to Bermuda in a most dilapidated condition, and as I was the only one who could speak English, the captain asked me to go ashore with the papers. The sea was running high, and, as the small boat turned in between the headlands toward the harbor, the high waves swamped us. We clung to the boat, and, as luck would have it, a launch came along just then and picked us up. After we had refitted at Bermuda, we sailed away toward New York, and finally reached here in March. I liked the sea and I liked adventure, and so the voyage did not seem as bad as it might have been."

"You should put that voyage in a story," I suggested, thinking of some of Kipling's tales of the sea; and it is curious, by the way, that Mr. Crawford, with all his love of the sea, has never written a regular sea-story, although there are several chapters in "Dr. Claudius" describing an ocean voyage.

It was about this time, when he was twenty-seven years of age, that Mr. Crawford entered Harvard as a special student, and took Professor Lanman's course in Sanskrit. He lived between New York and Boston, sometimes in one city and sometimes in the other, from December, 1882, to May, 1883, and contributed special articles to periodicals. He wrote book reviews and articles on philosophical themes. "I got so far," he said, "as to receive one hundred dollars for an article. Of course it was a precarious living, but there was always Uncle Sam (Samuel Ward) to whom I could go."

"And now tell me," I said, "the true story of how you came to write 'Mr. Isaacs.' I have read different versions of it."

"It has once or twice been told correctly," said Mr. Crawford, "and this is exactly how it happened: On May 5, 1882, Uncle Sam asked me to dine with him at the New York Club, which was then in the building on Madison Square, now called the Madison Square Bank Building. It goes without saying that we had a good dinner if it was ordered by Uncle Sam. We had dined rather early, and were sitting in the smoking-room, overlooking Madison Square, while it was still light. As was perfectly natural we began to exchange stories while smoking, and I told him, with a great deal of detail, my recollections of an interesting man whom I had met in Simla. When I had finished he said to me, 'That is a good two-part magazine story, and you must write it out immediately.' He took me around to his apartments, and that night I began to write the story of 'Mr. Isaacs.' Part of the first chapter was written afterward, but the rest of that chapter and several succeeding chapters are the story that I told to Uncle Sam. I kept at it from day to day, getting more interested in the work as I proceeded, and from time to time I would read a chapter to Uncle Sam. When I got through the original story, I was so amused with the writing of it that it occurred to me that I might as well make *Mr. Isaacs* fall in love with an English girl, and then I kept on writing, to see what would happen. By and by I remembered a mysterious Buddhist whom I had once met in India, and so I introduced him, to still further complicate matters. I went to Newport to visit my aunt, Mrs. Julia Ward Howe, while I was in the midst of the story, and continued it there. It was on June 13, 1882, while in her home, that I finished the last chapter of ' Mr. Isaacs ; ' and, Uncle Sam appearing in Newport at that time, I read him the part of the story which he had not heard. 'You will give it to me,' he said ; ' I shall try and find a publisher.' He had for many years frequented the book-store of Macmillan, and was well acquainted with the elder George Brett. He took the manuscript to Mr. Brett, who forwarded it to the English house, and in a short time it was accepted.''

"Having tasted blood," said Mr. Crawford, "I began, very soon after finishing ' Mr. Isaacs,' to write another story for my own amusement—' Dr. Claudius.' Late in November I was advised by Messrs. Macmillan that in order to secure an English, as well as an American, copyright, I must be on English soil on the day of publication. So I went to St. John, New Brunswick, where I had a very pleasant time, and continued to write the story of 'Dr. Claudius,' which I finished in December. 'Mr. Isaacs' was published on December 6th, and I, of course, knew nothing about its reception. However, toward the end of the month, I started on my return journey to the United States, and when I arrived in Boston, on the day before Christmas, and stepped out of the train, I was surprised beyond measure to find the railway news-stands almost covered with great posters announcing 'Mr. Isaacs.' The next morning, at my hotel, I found a note awaiting me from T. B. Aldrich, then editor of the *Atlantic Monthly*, asking me for an interview, at which he proposed that I write a serial for his magazine. I felt confident then, and do now, that 'Dr. Claudius' would not be a good serial story. However, I promised that he should have a serial, and began soon after to write 'The Roman Singer,' which was completed in February, 1883."

This led me to ask Mr. Crawford about the rapidity with which he worked. "I was told the other day," I said, "that you wrote 'The Three Fates' in seven days."

"No," he replied; "that would have been a physical impossibility. As a matter of fact, I was not very well, and spent a whole summer writing it from time to time. One of my stories, however, 'Marzio's Crucifix,' which is not a long novel, I wrote in ten days, in its original form, as it appeared serially. Afterward two chapters were added for book publication. 'The Tale of a Lonely Parish' I wrote in twenty-four days—one chapter a day, of about five thousand words. Both of those stories were easy to write, because I was perfectly familiar with the background of each. I had once studied silver-carving with a skilled workman, and the idea suggested itself to me to write a story about an atheist who should put his life and soul into the carving of a crucifix. With that for a motive, the story wrote itself. In the case of 'The Lonely Parish,' I found myself with a promise unredeemed, given to my publishers, for a novel at a certain date; I had already sold the novel which I intended for them to a magazine for serial publication. So I looked around in my memory for some spot which was thoroughly familiar to me as a background for my novel—so familiar that I need not invent details, but simply call them up from my memory. I immediately thought of the little village of Hatfield Regis, in Hertfordshire, where I was sent as a pupil to a clergyman. I lifted that little village bodily out of my memory, and put it into my story, even to the extent of certain real names and localities."

The life of Mr. Crawford, from the success of "Mr. Isaacs" to the present day, has been one of hard literary work. He sailed for Italy in May, 1883, spent most of the year 1884 in Constantinople, where he was married to a daughter of General Berdan, and in 1885 went back to Italy and to Sorrento, where his villa is, and where he has lived ever since, with the exception of his visits to America in 1893–5.

In these thirteen years he has produced twenty-five novels, and his popularity continues unabated.

"What," I asked, "is the germ of a novel for you?"

"It is a character, and not a situation, which generally suggests a novel to me. I think that in most cases my characters are portraits of real people in imaginary situations; that is why they cannot be recognized by the originals, because they are out of their usual environment. There are two exceptions to this way of conceiving a novel; as I have already told you, 'The Tale of a Lonely Parish' and 'Marzio's Crucifix' were suggested to me by the real background."

"Won't you tell me," I asked, "how you go to work to construct a novel?"

"Since my first novel or two, I always see the end of the story from the start. When I have thought it over in this way, I take a large sheet of paper, and, having decided on the size of the book, I make up my mind that it shall have—say twenty-four chapters. Along the left margin I mark the numbers of these chapters, one under the other, a line for each. If it is to be in three volumes, as most of my novels are in England, I place a horizontal mark after each eight chapter numbers. That indicates the volume. Then, after the manner of a playwright choosing what he calls his 'curtain situation,' I decide on the culminating incident in each volume, and also decide in which chapter it shall fall, and place a catchword indicating that situation on the line with the chapter number. Then I fill in for the other chapters a catchword or phrase which indicates the minor incidents in succession that culminate in the major incident. Of course all these things do not come at once, and I may fill in, from time to time, after I have begun the novel. But when the skeleton is comparatively complete, I begin to work. Along the right-hand margin I write down the calendar of the novel, as it may be called, from day to day. If it is a novel in which the action takes place in a very short time, I write down not only the day of the month and week, but the hour of the day, so that the action of the story may move logically. With this skeleton of the novel before me, I write with great rapidity. I have found that if I write a novel slowly my conception of the leading characters may change from week to week, so that in the end the novel is not so forcible or so complete as those written rapidly."

"Do you ever dictate?" I asked.

"I dictated one novel under stress of circumstances, and I do not think that I shall ever dictate another, for I consider it a relative failure."

"You are oftenest thought of, I think, as the author of the Saracinesca group of stories. Could you tell me how you planned them?"

"I think the origin of the stories was a walk I took, in the interior of Italy, with a tutor, when I was a boy—the region in which I have placed the Saracinesca estates. When I wrote the first novel of the series I did not intend a group; but the plan grew upon me, and the first story was received so kindly that I decided to continue the history through several generations, and make it, in a sense, representative of the life of the nobility of a certain class in modern Italy."

"You have been writing a group of New York novels, in which the fortunes of a family are elaborated after the manner of your Saracinesca series?"

"Yes; I worked very hard at the group, and the first of the series, 'Katharine Lauderdale,' has already gone through many editions. The second is called 'The Ralstons.' Some of the characters also appear in my little novel of Bar Harbor, 'Love in Idleness.' In 'Casa Braccio,' I have introduced characters from both the Italian and American groups of novels."

This ended our conversation. The impression left on my mind was of delightful converse with a virile, strong, intellectual man, whose imagination and emotions are the obedient servants of a dominating will; above all things, a man of the world in the best sense, and a scholar in the best sense, whose knowledge is a delight to him, whose contact with people in great cities has broadened and deepened his serious views of life; a man with that poise of body and mind which assures one that at forty his work as a novelist has hardly reached maturity, but that the best of it lies in the future.

HENRY VAN DYKE

IF you walk across the campus under the old elms at Princeton, almost any night of the spring or fall terms, you will probably hear somewhere a group or marching body of students singing, to the tune of " Marching through Georgia "—

> " Nassau ! Nassau ! Ring out the chorus free.
> Nassau ! Nassau ! Thy jolly sons are we.
> Cares shall be forgotten, all our sorrows flung away,
> While we are marching thro' Princeton ! "

Most of the fun which Princeton students have had in the past twenty years has been enjoyed to the words of this song, written by Henry van Dyke, of the Class of '73. Since that time he has turned his attention to other things, and has been hard at work for fifteen years as the minister of two large churches, one at Newport and one in New York. Of course it is hardly fair to hold Dr. van Dyke responsible for all the revels which his song has inspired ; but a strict Calvinist cannot refrain from putting it on record that any account of the life and works of Dr. van

Dyke which does not take this song into the reckoning is incomplete.

It is a good song, at any rate, for the reason that Dr. van Dyke has always been a wholesome man. It is hard to spoil a man who has always been fond of hunting and fishing and the free life of the woods. Three years at a theological seminary can't drive that out of a man, especially if his father was fond of the same things and taught him to love them.

"I have fished from Norway to the Nile," he recently said, "and the only kind of hunting I do not like is heresy-hunting."

I asked him for a "basis of facts" from which I could start to build up a character for him, and he replied:

"On reflection I am chagrined to discover how few facts there are in my personal history—unless you propose to count as facts the fish caught from the age of five to the present time."

I tried to talk theology with him one afternoon in order to discover whether I could approve of his Presbyterianism, but he switched the talk over to fishing for land-locked salmon at the Grande Décharge, and closed the theological discussion with the story of catching three brook trout in Lily Bay, up in Maine, that weighed eleven pounds.

That is why I can't give his views on the inerrancy of the Scriptures in this sketch. But I do know, for he has stated it with emphasis, that he has been trying "to do his part in keeping elbow-room for a healthy mind in the Presbyterian Church—believing that a little modest ignorance is the best foundation for a sound theology."

Every one who lives in New York knows that Dr. van Dyke is doing this very successfully in the historic old Brick Church at the corner of Fifth Avenue and Thirty-seventh Street. He has gathered around him there a strong congregation of refined people, who are interested in the æsthetic problems of living as well as the moral. For, so far as I can judge, the aim of Dr. Van Dyke's preaching and writing is to lead people to live full, healthy, and rational lives —with due regard to truth and beauty, as well as goodness. He has, I think, put a great deal of his creed into the dedication of his volume on "The Poetry of Tennyson:"

To a Young Woman of an Old Fashion, who loves Art, not for its own sake, but because it ennobles life; who reads Poetry not to kill time but to fill it with beautiful thoughts; and who still believes in God and Duty and Immortal Love.

In one of his books he says, "A short creed well believed and honestly applied is what we need. The world waits, and we must pray and labor, not for a more complete and logical Theology, but for a more real and true and living Christianity."

He put it all in a nutshell one day when we were talking, when he said: "It's better to live than to write about life."

As a literary man Dr. van Dyke has received the

widest recognition for "The Poetry of Tennyson," which is not only a careful study of the technic of the poet, but in a much broader way is an interpretation of the views of art and life with which the poems abound. Tennyson appealed to him because his poems "voiced the great reaction out of the heart of a doubting age, toward the Christianity of Christ and the trust in Immortal Love." This volume met with the warmest approval from the poet himself, who furnished material to make the second edition more complete. During the last summer of his life, at the laureate's express wish, Dr. van Dyke visited him in England, and received his cordial thanks for his sympathetic interpretation.

Another volume which has been welcomed with great favor is "The Christ-Child in Art," which is a commentary on the work of the masters in painting who have portrayed the Madonna and Child.

He has also written a number of allegorical stories of unusual beauty in diction, and most graceful in fancy, among them "The Oak of Geismar" and "The Source" in *Scribner's*, and "The Story of the Other Wise Man" in *Harper's*. Some day he will put these, with other stories, in a volume which will gain for him recognition in another literary field.

Dr. van Dyke's volumes of distinctly religious import are "The Reality of Religion" (1884), "The Story of the Psalms" (1887), and "Straight Sermons" (1893). And of equal moral importance might be mentioned his yellow-covered tract on the copyright question which was entitled "The Sin of Literary Piracy."

To any one still hungering for a "basis of facts" about Dr. van Dyke, it may be said that he is the son of the late Henry J. van Dyke, for so many years pastor of the First Presbyterian Church in Brooklyn. He was born November 10, 1852, in Germantown, Pa., just "two hundred years after the arrival of his ancestor, Jan Thomasse van Dyke, in this country," and he is, therefore, "Dutch as Holland." He was graduated at the Brooklyn Polytechnic Institute in 1869, at Princeton College in 1873, and Princeton Theological Seminary in 1877. He further studied philosophy and theology in Berlin under Weiss, Dorner, and Harms. He was pastor of the United Congregational Church, Newport, R. I., in 1879–82, and in 1883 came to the old Brick Church in New York. Princeton gave him the degree of D.D. in 1884. Harvard elected him University Preacher for 1890–92, and he was appointed to the Lyman Beecher lectureship at Yale for 1895–96.

ARCADIAN OPINIONS

SUMMER READING

WHY should anyone read books for amusement in summer? Amusement is a matter of choice, until riches make of it a profession. Of course for the very rich amusement and pleasure are simply the synonyms of spending money agreeably. That usually implies the spending of it ostentatiously or in a way to arouse the envy of those less fortunate. But the well-to-do man or woman of scant or moderate leisure cannot afford to take envy into account as one of the forms of amusement. And it usually happens that they are the very people who put a few books in a corner of their luggage when they start off to camp or the seashore for a breathing spell. If you ask them why, they always say that it may rain for a day or two, and moreover the days are so long!

Can anyone imagine the days being too long for a dweller in the city who has only one month of the twelve in which to loose himself from the routine of living! The trouble is with that very routine to which his nerves have become so adjusted that they respond with pleasure to it alone. When it isn't pursued he misses it, just as he misses his wife, whom he knows he has unhappily married. But then he has become used to her particular way of quarrelling, and his faculties respond to it with alertness.

It is the same way with reading. He was brought up to believe that there was some particular virtue in a book; that it had an intimate connection with what was called "improvement of the mind." So when he had leisure he went for a book, as a toper for whiskey. By and by he found that it made him "forget things," and he accumulated his little likes and dislikes for various authors as he would for brands of cigars. When he got that far he believed that he had acquired "taste" in reading, and perhaps he began to accumulate a library as he would a wine-cellar.

So when he goes off for a summer vacation you will see him, on a rainy day in camp, pull out a book and go at it with the complacency of a man who knows he is doing his duty. There may be half a dozen interesting men in camp who have seen a great deal of the world near at hand. He never looks on them as an opportunity. He would rather read a book by some interesting invalid who likes to put her sensations on paper, than talk with a man who had slain wild beasts in a jungle, or ran for sheriff in a Western mining-camp.

Most contemporary books (except as repositories of valuable information) are merely substitutes for entertaining men and women, and usually very poor substitutes. Your manner of life may make it necessary for you to enlarge your horizon principally by books when at home; but when you are away from the old surroundings, if you are the wise man you think you are, you will leave your books at home and try to meet some new types of the human animal. It may make you more contented with your own way of life to discover how many worse kinds there are.

"SANT' ILARIO" IN CAMP

ONE'S recollection of a book is composite—part the impression made by the literary creation, and part by the circumstances under which it was read. Many a dull book becomes a pleasant memory, and a work of genius perhaps is associated with pain.

To think of Crawford's "Sant' Ilario," recalls a rainy day at Cedar Island Camp. The foreground of the memory is the streets and squares of modern Rome; the background is a broad gray surface of water stretching off to a shore covered with stately cedars, poplars, and balsams. As in a cyclorama, it is hard to distinguish where Rome ends and the Adirondack lake begins. You know that the beautiful *Corona* lived in the stately Palazzo Saracinesca, and you half believe that in one corner of that palace there is a long, narrow room with a wolf-skin stretched on the wall, and two bucks' heads on either side. And outside there is a rustic piazza with rubber coats, and guns, and fishing-tackle hanging on the logs.

Through the open door you hear men's voices—laughter and blunt repartee, with a story now and then. Somehow you cannot quite determine whether

Sant' Ilario, *Gouache*, and *San Giacinto*, are having a game of poker or whether it is the three guides. You are sure, however, that the game is being played by the correct American rules. The excitement deepens; you are absorbed in the story, and feel that a great crisis has been reached when the Garibaldians and Papal troops have a battle while the fate of a "jack-pot" is being determined. You hold your breath as the Papal soldiers charge up the hill, and are ready to break into cheers at the bravery of the solitary figure on a rampart tearing down the stone wall while the bullets strike all around him. With his fate still in doubt, you hear a shout of triumph, and learn that "four trays" have been successfully played against "three bullets," and that the "jack-pot" had been "scooped by Abner"—to use the elegant phrase which lingers in your ear.

This victory overshadows the battle of the Papal troops, and increases in importance with later reports that "Ab has cleaned up both the Old Man and Iry."

Then night comes down with the pouring rain. All dwellers in the Adirondacks are divided into two classes—Guides and Sports—and both classes gather around the roaring fire. You join the circle, and in the quiet of an after-dinner smoke float off to Rome and the Saracinesca. The fate of the beautiful *Faustina* is becoming engrossing, when the Old Man breaks the silence with a bear story. Mr. Crawford cannot hold his own as a teller of stories with an intelligent Adirondack guide. You soon leave *Faustina* in prison to follow the veteran guide into a bear's cave; or to go on a trail with him through the forest after a bear that ran so fast that he left the mark of his stomach in the light snow at every jump. "There ain't no dog in these parts can catch them on a dead run," he said to the incredulous.

When the stories are ended you go to sleep in a bark cottage by the edge of the lake, and dream that *Sant' Ilario* is watching for deer with you in the flow-ground; that you push the boat on a marsh island, and build a little fire of twigs and rushes; that while the hounds are baying along the hillside, *Sant' Ilario* and you are discussing the next move of Garibaldi, and plotting to release the beautiful *Faustina* from prison. Two shots down by Windmill Point startle you! "That was *Gouache* shooting the deer," says *Sant' Ilario*. Then you hear the clear, sharp whistle of the huntsman calling in the hounds, and you know that the chase is ended.

Together you row through the dead and spectral-like trees of the flow-ground, and out into the open lake. Soon you land on *Windmill Point*.

"Where is the big buck?" you ask. And in your dream you do not know whether it is *Gouache* or Abner who replies:

"It's a yearlin' doe. We robbed the cradle."

The dream is prophetic of the great hunt on which you start that day. In the evening a huge fire of roots and knots is built in front of the open camp.

It is a gloomy, rainy night, but the camp is a cheery place. You sit on a bed of spruce boughs and watch the swaying flames — imagining that *Montevarchi*, *Giovanni*, and the rest are sitting in the shadow.

"What do you think of 'Sant' Ilario?'" is asked from a cloud of smoke which may belong to *Gouache's* pipe.

"It has given me so much pleasure," you say, "and is so interwoven with our experiences on this beautiful lake that I cannot express a critical opinion. All I know is that it made a rainy day in camp seem short. For me it is hereafter a part of Cedar Island; and when I smell the odor of spruce, or am awakened by the music of waters, I shall at once think of 'Sant' Ilario.'"

A LEGEND OF THE HAPPY VALLEY

MIDWAY between the crisp air and keen intelligence of the North and the lazy breezes of the impulsive South, there is a Happy Valley. It lies in the sheltering arms of two beautiful mountain ranges: the North Mountain peaks are blue and rugged, standing out against the sky with bare, wrinkled, masculine brows; but the South Mountain is a long, wavy line of soft, feminine curves, clad from head to foot in rich velvet—dark and green. The dwellers in the Happy Valley have long believed that they are watched over by two good Spirits: the genius of the North Mountain is a stern but benignant old man, while the South Mountain is the home of a gracious woman, full of charity and tenderness. Whether the people in the Valley are happy because these kind Spirits really exist, or merely because they *believe* in their existence, has never been determined by the sages who live there. They are content to know that the force of the North wind is broken before it reaches them, and that the scorching sirocco is cooled as it glides over the brow of the Southern hills.

One Christmas Eve, very long ago, the good Spirits

looked down on the Valley, which was filled with laughter, good-will, and song that rose up like a flood to the very tops of the mountains, and overflowed into the country beyond.

But there was one gloomy young man there, who sat in a room filled with shadows, and looked out upon a hill-top where the light of the stars showed a windrow of snow on the grave of his best friend.

"How shall we bring cheer to him on Christmas Day?" asked the good Spirits of each other; and far into the night they debated the question, sending messages back and forth so frequently that belated men thought the air was filled with snow.

The old man on the North Mountain insisted that Wisdom would be his best comforter, but the Hamadryad of the South was equally convinced of the power of Love. The end of the long discussion was a compromise, by which both Wisdom and Love were to be offered to the sorrowful young man on Christmas Day.

So it happened that on the morrow the young man's Boston uncle sent him the Best Hundred Books, and his cousin from Virginia arrived, accompanied with a beautiful daughter, whose eyes were like the depths of a pine forest when the sunlight sifts through the boughs.

For five years the young man was absent from the Happy Valley. He loved much, he read many books, he travelled and studied in many lands; and when he came home again on Christmas Eve, with wife and children, men called him wise. He was back in the old home, in the shadow-haunted room, looking out in the starlight upon the grave on the hill. Again the good mountain Spirits looked down upon the Valley and saw his face. There was no gloom in it, neither was there great joy. They could not read the riddle of his countenance, and they filled the air above the Valley with their vain questions.

"Come," said the rugged old Genie of the North, "let us go down into the Valley and talk with this young man who has lived and suffered. We have dwelt on the mountain tops so long that we are out of touch with Humanity."

"I will go with you," said the gentle Hamadryad, "though sympathy and love have always kept me nearer than you to the hearts of the people. My mountain tops are not in the clouds."

So together they drifted into the presence of the young man—strange forms of "mingled mist and light."

"Five years ago I started you on the way of Wisdom," said the grizzled old Genie. "Then you were in the shadow of a great sorrow; now I think I see you filled with peace. Tell us—is Wisdom, then, the royal road to happiness?"

When the young man raised his eyes they were full of doubts and ambitions, struggling at the windows of his mind for glimpses of the light. "My friend," he said, "you started me upon an arduous journey.

I have toiled on through fog and marsh, without once feeling sure that I was upon the right way. I only know that I have a stouter heart than when I started, and I have courage left to cheer those who reach out their hands to me from the darkness."

"But my gift of Love," said the Hamadryad; "surely it brought you more of happiness and joy than this?"

"Love," said the young man, "was a precious gift, but it has doubled fate's opportunities to do me harm. Now, more than ever, am I the football of chance, and my capacity for suffering is increased. Love has brought me many things, but not happiness."

"What, then," said the good Spirits together, "have Love and Wisdom brought you that are worth the having?"

"Hope!" he said, while the light of a new day was creeping in at the window and brightening his tired face, "not for myself, but for——"

"Merry Christmas!" the children shouted in glee, as the door swung suddenly open. Their faces were radiant with hope, and in *them* was the promise of the future. The Genie and the Hamadryad showered blessings on them as they vanished toward the mountain tops.

A PLEA FOR "DIANA"

A MEMORY OF THE LIGHTHOUSE AT MONTEREY.

THE lighthouse-keeper led them through a neatly furnished room or two, up an easy stairway, and then abruptly to a perpendicular ladder, at the top of which there was a square of clear, blue sky—"a silky blue," said Adrian, "like a Yale banner at the top of a coach on a football day." When he reached the last rung of the ladder and stepped out onto the breezy platform around the great sea-light, the silken banner had become an immeasurable dome of luminous blue, without a fleck or spot of any other color.

As Dupont pulled his rotund body through the narrow opening and stood in the bright sunlight he found breath to say:

"Ah, Adrian, my friend, I now appreciate how Dante felt when he had reached the top of the mountain of Purgatory and emerged upon the beautiful Terrestrial Paradise, and Virgil said to him:

> "'Beyond the steep ways and the narrow art thou;
> Behold the sun that shines upon thy forehead;
> Behold the grass, the flowers, and the shrubs,
> Which of itself alone this land produces!'"

"If I am playing Virgil to your Dante on this trip to Monterey," said Adrian, "I must remind you that it was on the borders of the Terrestrial Paradise that Virgil said good-by and left Dante to the fascinations of Matilda and Beatrice. See, there is one of them now, going across the fields to St. Mary's-by-the-Sea—

'A lady all alone, who went along
Singing and culling floweret after floweret,
With which her pathway was all painted over.'

Can you believe that this is Christmas Day; that Matilda there is going to her devotions in midwinter, clothed in white lawn and culling poppies by the way; that yesterday we were shivering on the peaks of the Sierras, and to-day we are fanning ourselves by the Pacific? No, Dante, Virgil made a huge error in leaving you at the edge of the Terrestrial Paradise! I propose to stay—at least till Beatrice appears. I warn you I can't endure Beatrice, with the everlasting 'splendor of her laughing eyes.' Dante may have been deeply in love with Beatrice, but it has always seemed strange to me that he remembered no other feature than her eyes. I think of her as one of those uninteresting women who make their eyes do duty for wit, intelligence, and vivacity."

"We are too old for such as Beatrice, Adrian. At our age the only woman in the world is like *Diana of The Crossways*."

"There you are again with one of George Meredith's heroines! From the Gotham Club to the tennis grounds at Del Monte I have had the journey across the continent decorated with eulogies of Meredith."

"Come, Adrian, be honest. Confess that since we left Salt Lake your trips to the smoking-car have been made to elude my ridicule while you read *Diana*."

"I see there is no escape from you, Dupont. Either we must discuss *Diana*, or separate, like Virgil and Dante, on Christmas Day."

"It can't be helped. That stretch of dimpling, sunny water there, across the bay to Santa Cruz, reminds me irresistibly of *Diana*—with 'all her face one tender sparkle of a smile.'"

"Go on," said Adrian. "Your admiration for Meredith is a mania which can only be cured by giving it free vent."

"Well, then, I'll give you an unreasonable superlative to start with. To me *Diana Warwick* is among the few irresistible women of fiction. Other writers may tell you over and over again that a woman is witty, fascinating, intelligent in every motion of her mind. Meredith does a much more difficult thing—he *shows* you the wit and intelligence, and leaves you to judge of its quality. He is one of the few writers who do not resort to generalizations to conceal their poverty in invention."

"If you please, my friend," said the skeptical Adrian, "what became of Meredith's power of invention when he had once launched so fine a character as *Diana Merion?* I believe that he broke down in the middle of the story. From *Diana's* night-watch to the end of the tale is a disappointing anti-climax." Then Adrian blew fleecy whirls of smoke toward the stainless sky, and serenely leaned over the railing and looked out to the far horizon, waiting for the inevitable explosion.

Dupont was used to this form of baiting. It was understood between them that if they travelled together they must disagree about everything except the itinerary of the journey. The wise Adrian often said: " Imagine two people whose minds are in similar grooves starting out on a vacation together! One might as well carry a mirror for company and entertainment."

" You know you are unfair, Adrian," said Dupont, warming up, as a true disciple. " You persist in belittling a great writer of English fiction because his vocabulary worries you. But there is *Diana*, my boy, from the first page to the last a creature of beauty and variety, and more charming under calumny than other women whose reputations are unassailed. What you call the anti-climax of the story is the most subtile and natural development of a complex character. It is not *Diana* who should be blamed for falling from her ideal, but a rotten social system which forced her into a false position."

" You assail a whole class of society in order to praise a woman who in Egypt would have been a Cleopatra."

" That is too severe. *Diana* was what *Sir Lukin* called her—'the loyalest woman anywhere.' He pictured her completely in one of his brusque sentences: 'She's man and woman in brains, and legged like a deer, and breasted like a swan, and a regular sheaf of arrows in her eyes. Her one error was that marriage of hers.' "

"*Sir Lukin* and you have pointed the way to her greatest fault," said Adrian. " If she had been the right sort of woman she would have made a charming husband out of *Warwick* instead of wrecking his life. He had the stuff of an English gentleman in him."

" He had inherited the prejudices of six or eight generations of social prigs, and he never could have appreciated a bright and starry spirit like *Diana*."

" She was weak, vain, emotional, and, like most women, betrayed the first important secret that was entrusted to her," said Adrian.

" She was sincere, affectionate, and benevolent. She tried hard to make a bright corner in a cruel world which loves falsehood and the dark. I'll admit she failed, wofully and disastrously; but on a Christmas Day like this, when your altruism ought to come to the surface, you should give credit to her idealism. The failure of such a woman is not anticlimax. I like to think of *Tom Redworth* as the happiest of men with *Diana* as his wife. The mistletoe hanging to that tree over there by the roadside calls up a Christmas picture in great contrast to this fragrant, flower-scented place. I can see The Crossways on the Downs, covered with snow — a bleak and wintry English landscape. But beyond the threshold of the Crossways you enter into warmth, cheeriness, good-fellowship. The rooms are decked with mistletoe and holly; *Emmy's* godchild is dancing in joy before a tree hung with the treasures of fairy-land; in the library *Sir Lukin, Redworth, Arthur Rhodes, Whitmonby,* and *Harry Wilmers* are tossing wit and story back and forth, feathered with laughter. And on the hearth before the grate kneels *Diana*, with the 'first-fire glow' touching her features as it did one bleak night, years ago. Now, as then, *Redworth* imagines her 'a Madonna on an old black Spanish canvas.' She is holding the hand of a sweet-faced invalid, who rests beside her in an easy-chair, and I believe it is that blessed woman, *Emmy*, who still serenely lingers 'on the dark decline of the unillumined verge between the two worlds.' Outside, the Christmas bells are ringing."

"Come, Dupont, you have been dreaming," said Adrian. "Those are the chimes in the old tower of Carmello Mission, brought a century ago from Spain. Let me call you back to this continent with these lines of Stevenson's:

"'Now that you have spelt your lesson, lay it down and go and play,
Seeking shells and seaweed on the sands of Monterey;
Watching all the mighty whalebones lying buried by the breeze,
Tiny sandypipers, and the huge Pacific Seas.'"

A CURE FOR THE MALADY OF CLEVERNESS

THERE has been a good deal of moralizing on the death of Dr. Holmes as closing a notable period in American letters, with lamentations over the present decadence through the malady of "cleverness." The young men who are writing these lamentations are suffering from this same malady of cleverness themselves. It is one of the prerogatives of cleverness to "sass" its contemporaries—particularly if they are American. The proper thing is to be so civilized that you appreciate the art and letters of all countries except your own. When Dr. Holmes was young he became one of a coterie of other young men who believed in their country and in themselves and in each other. Of course all that was very provincial from our point of view. They ought to have spent their youth and enthusiasm in telling each other how very crude they were; that the place to learn to write poetry was England, and fiction, France. Instead of Longfellow's writing in admiration of Hawthorne in the *North American* at a time when he needed praise, he ought to have pointed out how very narrow and provincial were all the "Twice-told Tales," with no glimpse in them of anything beyond a New England village. Longfellow could have done that beautifully, for he had been "abroad" and knew a thing or two. But all of those young men believed in being genuine American writers rather than imitation foreign ones. They took the material nearest their hands and hearts, and made the most of it.

When you get down to the bottom of it, you'll probably conclude that there was a pretty fine moral quality back of all their optimism that put fire into their writings—and that was "loyalty," a virtue of which little is said nowadays, except during political campaigns. It used to mean a man of honest convictions and attachments to which he stuck through evil and good report. It gave a unity and stability to his career, whether he was a mechanic or a poet. There was and is a steadying quality about loyalty which frees a man from a host of unnecessary worries and apprehensions, and keeps him young in spirit and enthusiasm.

All of which is no excuse for the prejudices of ignorance. Holmes and his contemporaries were men who tried to know something of the best that was being done in the world; but they believed in applying that knowledge *in* and *for* America.

There is one thing strongly in favor of the clever young men of to-day—and that is their health of body and mind. The spread of college and amateur athletics has had a great deal to do with it. A large part of their cynicism is simply disgust with the morbid introspection of the school of American writers which prevailed a few years ago. A healthy young man is likely to say that it is "all rot"—and he is pretty nearly right about it. He is beginning to write some books to please himself, and they are full of the enthusiasm of health. They are, perhaps, a little materialistic, which is natural, for youth is material in its motives.

A good healthy organism will be pleased with its surroundings, or at least see what is good in them. By and by these healthy young writers will begin to see and write about what is best in their own country; and then all their cynicism will vanish like a mist. They will be surprised to see how their own countrymen will buy their books, and talk about them. For the American is more anxious to think well of his country than the American newspaper or novelist will permit him to think.

THE PATRIOTIC NOVEL

THE flags were flying the other day on all the high buildings in the city, to signify that it was the birthday of a patriot. It was a beautiful day, and, as the flags fluttered against the blue, solid citizens raised their eyes from the streets, and felt a little tremor in their hearts, especially if they were over forty and recalled what intense emotions the flag stood for when they were in their youth.

But the bulk of the people on the streets were under thirty, and to them the flag is a symbol of merrymakings—a fetich that clubs and hotels and theatres display on days that are devoted to pleasure. They associate it somehow with picnics of the John J. O'Malley Association, which is organized for spoils; with parades of grizzled veterans who, the cynical assert, are organized for pension raids; or, with the topmost girl in the closing spectacle of a ballet or comic opera.

The boy from the country has still another association with the flag—the rural cemetery where a score or more of graves are marked with little weather-stained flags that set apart the resting-places of patriots.

Even for him the flag stands for a day of fun, for an incongruous procession where marched all the odd characters of the village, and a hay-wagon covered with bunting in which rode the local beauties, gorgeous in white muslin with red and blue sashes, and carrying wreaths of flowers.

And for old and young alike who read the papers there is somewhere in a cranny of the mind a well-defined idea that the flag nowadays is a symbol of political bluster, and that the modern patriot is the man who goes to Congress " for the glory of the old flag and an appropriation."

There is nothing in the fiction or general literature of the decade to counteract this decay of patriotism as a sentiment. Indeed the men of judgment and education are rather afraid of the sentimental side of it—it has been associated with so much that is impractical, wrong-headed, and hypocritical. When the patriot creeps into our fiction at all, it is to be made fun of, to be shown up as a ludicrous person, or a rather awkward knave. Our novelists would rather analyze the perturbations of the heart of an immature girl, or the rascalities of a " gilded youth," than show us the development of the character of a really patriotic man, who stands in his community for integrity, fidelity, enthusiasm in all things relating to his country, his state, his own town, his home. He is not dead by any means, for almost every hamlet has him in some stage of development. He stands for the best Americanism, and the encouraging thing is that he has the respect and often the admiration of the community in which he lives. That is strong enough proof that the country at large knows real patriotism when it sees it.

But surely it ought to be in our fiction! French, German, and Italian novels are permeated with it—for their novelists realize that they are appealing to the strongest passion, but one, in the breast of man. Looked at merely from the side of Art, we ought to have more of it, for it is inspiring, elevating, often dramatic.

And then it is clean, and decent, and manly—and a big-brained man can feel that he is not engaged in the work of a " woman-novelist " if he writes a really patriotic novel.

www.ingramcontent.com/pod-product-compliance
Lightning Source LLC
Chambersburg PA
CBHW030247170426
43202CB00009B/652